lessons of disaster

American Governance and Public Policy series
Series Editors: Gerald W. Boychuk, Karen Mossberger, and Mark C. Rom

lessons of disaster

POLICY CHANGE AFTER
CATASTROPHIC EVENTS

THOMAS A. BIRKLAND

Georgetown University Press
Washington, D.C.

As of January 1, 2007, 13-digit ISBN numbers will replace the current 10-digit system.
Paperback: 978-1-58901-121-2
Cloth: 978-1-58901-120-5

Georgetown University Press, Washington, D.C.

Library of Congress Cataloging-in-Publication Data

Birkland, Thomas A.
  Lessons of disaster : policy change after catastrophic events / Thomas A. Birkland.
      p. cm. — (American governance and public policy series)
  Includes bibliographical references and index.
      ISBN 1-58901-120-1 (hardcover : alk. paper) — ISBN 1-58901-121-X (pbk. : alk. paper)
  1. Political planning—United States. 2. Policy sciences. 3. Emergency management—Government policy—United States—Case studies. 4. Disaster relief—Government policy—United States—Case studies. 5. Natural disasters —Government policy—United States—Case studies. 6. Aeronautics—Safety measures—Government policy—United States—Case studies. I. Title.
  II. Series: American governance and public policy.

JK468.P64B585 2006
363.34′5610973—dc22   2006003282

This book is printed on acid-free paper meeting the requirements of the American National Standard for Permanence in Paper for Printed Library Materials.

13 12 11 10 09 08 07 06   9 8 7 6 5 4 3 2
First printing

Printed in the United States of America

contents

illustrations

tables

figures

preface

This book was conceived in the year following the September 11 terrorist attacks on the United States. In the weeks that followed the attacks I was asked by friends, colleagues, students, and occasionally by journalists to explain the attacks and to put them into some sort of political or policy context. I sketched my initial thoughts in an opinion item written for a local newspaper, in which I argued that no matter how profound or frightening the attacks, our political system would accommodate a range of policy responses. The "system," I argued, would do its job. Certainly, terrorism and aviation security would be at the top of policymakers' agendas for the near future, but eventually other issues would gain attention (Birkland 2001).

When Barry Rabe, then editor of the series in which this book is published, and Gail Grella approached me with the idea for writing a follow-up to *After Disaster,* it seemed a natural way to expand more systematically on the argument of the earlier book. I argued there that big events have important but variable influences on policy agendas; in this book, I address the question of whether big events have the same influence on policy change. My claim that there would probably be sweeping policy change was based primarily on a belief that something as big as the September 11 attacks had to trigger *some* sort of policy change. Indeed, it did not take long for this educated guess to bear fruit; the president signed the USA PATRIOT Act on October 26, 2001, just slightly more than six weeks after the attacks. This was an usually fast pace for change in the American system, but the September 11 attacks were so unusual that they triggered such rapid policy change.

I also have a personal reason for my interest in terrorism as a form of disaster, and a personal reason for wanting to contribute, albeit in a small way, to making our nation less vulnerable to terrorist attacks. Before I entered academia, I worked in New Jersey government, and for one particularly interesting year I was a member of Governor Thomas Kean's staff in an office called the Authorities Unit. The Authorities Unit was charged with helping the governor keep track of the activities of various independent authorities, boards, and commissions that had been established to undertake many tasks, from running the toll roads to preserving farmland. One of my primary responsibilities was to track and analyze the activities of the Port Authority of New York and New Jersey (PA), the owner of the World Trade Center and operator of, among other things, the George Washington Bridge; the Lincoln and Holland tunnels; Newark, Kennedy, and LaGuardia airports; and, of particular interest here, the World Trade Center.

The politics behind the conception and building of the World Trade Center is a fascinating story, in large part because the Trade Center was often at the center of a sometimes cooperative, sometimes contentious relationship between two states (for two quite different views of the matter, see Darton 1999 and Gillespie 2002; for a more general history and analysis of the Port Authority, see Doig 2001). During my short tenure in the governor's office, many New York State offices were moving out of the World Trade Center. These offices paid very low rents, and with the Wall Street boom of the mid-1980s, the World Trade Center became more attractive to private tenants, who paid higher rents. The additional revenue thus generated exceeded what was pledged to bondholders, and a substantial part of my duties involved working with the PA and New York State to determine how to distribute what was at the time a financial windfall.

This project, and other business, required several meetings at the PA's executive headquarters in the north tower, 1 WTC, so

I became familiar with the remarkable complex of buildings and organizations contained in this rather compact corner of lower Manhattan. Like many New Yorkers and visitors, I never became fond of the *buildings* in the World Trade Center. They were generally utilitarian and architecturally undistinguished, and their public spaces could be cold and forbidding. Later, as the Battery Park city development grew at the foot of the towers—on landfill that was created from the soil excavated for the WTC's foundation—the stark verticality of the towers was softened somewhat. The familiar, undulating pattern of the Manhattan skyline was reestablished in lower Manhattan, the abruptness of the towers was muted, and people became fond of the *place* and of the symbol for which the towers stood. The towers loomed over downtown, serving in many ways as a familiar landmark and even a navigation aid for casual visitors to Manhattan. The views from the offices in the building were, of course, legendary—I found myself distracted at many meetings by chance sightings of the Brooklyn Bridge emerging from the fog, or of the Statue of Liberty in the distance, toward Staten Island. So I became fond of the place, taken by the sometimes wondrous moments afforded by the Twin Towers.

I teach at a public university in the state of New York, and the attack hit my university close to home. At least two alumni were killed on September 11, and several of my students, a large number of whom are from New York City, Long Island, and Westchester County, lost friends or family members in the attack, or knew someone who did. This attack, unlike many of the natural disasters I study, was not a distant event or a data point—it was something felt very deeply by New Yorkers and by other Americans and people around the world. In large part, this emotional response may be precisely what the perpetrators of this catastrophe sought. There is no way that anyone could call the attacks—and the collapse of the towers—an act of God or a tragic misfortune. Clearly, someone *intended* to kill thousands of people and do billions of dollars' worth of damage.

Given my personal interests and the foundation I laid in *After Disaster,* my path to writing this book seems clear. Of course, hundreds of books, articles, websites, photos, and other forms of media have been devoted to this event, and much more has yet to be written. I am particularly interested in the extent to which there are any "lessons" to be learned from September 11, both because there was so much discussion of "the lessons of September 11" and because the implicit mechanism of focusing events is that they reveal in some way the need for policy change. To assess the influence of September 11 on policy change and learning, I consider terrorism broadly in chapter 2, and then in chapter 3 I focus on aviation security as a central problem revealed by the September 11 attacks. It may overstate the case, but only slightly, to argue that had the aviation security system in general—and the security checkpoint screeners in particular—been successful in stopping at least some of the terrorists on September 11, the full extent of the tragedy might have been averted. What if cockpit doors were stronger? What if passenger profiling were effective, or even politically or normatively acceptable? These and other agonizing questions have been addressed in various places since September 11, sometimes by experts and often by kibitzers in the policy field, but the answers are unclear even if they are knowable. We do know that crimes against aviation date to the 1930s, with a major increase in terrorist (as opposed to merely criminal) activity in the 1960s and an increased use of bombs in the 1980s. As former governor Kean, the head of the 9/11 Commission, noted, the failure of responsible authorities to anticipate the hijacking and intentional destruction of airplanes was a "failure of imagination." Arguments that "we never imagined it could happen" are therefore specious because, as I show in chapters 2 and 3, there were people in government and the expert community who did imagine this kind of catastrophic terrorism.

I compare aviation security with two types of natural hazards, a prominent subject in *After Disaster*. My interest in natural hazards dates to my first graduate assistantship under Peter May at the University of Washington. The assistantship involved traveling throughout Washington State and interviewing local land-use planners about land uses and natural hazards. Later, natural hazards became a good complement to my interests in the hows and whys of the *Exxon Valdez* oil spill. These interests came together in *After Disaster*, and I continue to explore them in this book.

acknowledgments

Translating personal experience and curiosity into social science involves working with many people, and I am indebted to many friends and colleagues. Barry Rabe and Gail Grella initially planted the seed for this book, and I thank them for providing the opportunity to contribute a second book to this series. Karen Mossberger has been particularly helpful in challenging me to explain more clearly my arguments and their intellectual origins. Peter May has continued to be a patient mentor and critic. Regina Lawrence and George Busenberg have been generous colleagues who have enriched my knowledge of the media and of policy learning, respectively. Paul Sabatier and Chris Weible offered valuable comments on what was to become chapter 3. Patricia Strach, Sarah Michaels, Sara Anderson, and Sarah Pralle read the penultimate draft of the book and provided invaluable suggestions. Graduate students Jordan Slough and Norma Malfatti carefully edited the final draft and offered valuable comments. I also thank the staff at Georgetown University Press for their work on the book.

This book would not have been possible without the hard work of twenty-six remarkable undergraduate students in a special course I taught, "The September 11 Project," in the spring term of 2002. I offered this course so that students could explore their own understanding of the September 11 disaster, which touched many of them deeply. My goal in the course was to collect data on media coverage and legislation after September 11 and to test some hypotheses about how the media cover disasters of this magnitude. This way, students would learn more about the event and how social scientists study and help make sense of such events, both for themselves and for society as a whole. In many ways the sheer volume of the data—and the daily changes in politics and policy in early 2002—made this more an exercise in data collection than a project of generating and testing hypotheses, but my students learned a great deal about the vagaries of empirical research, and I learned a lot about my students. I am very grateful to them.

Three students in particular—Lisa Ferretti, Kathie Legg, and Jesse Matthewson—continued as research assistants after the class ended, aiding in collecting data for this and related projects on event-driven media coverage and policymaking. Paul Alexander, in my college's political science program, and Michael Deegan, in our Public Administration and Policy Department, were also important in gathering the evidence presented here. Deneen Hatmaker, a doctoral student in public administration, and Sara Anderson, a colleague at Albany, carefully read and commented on the manuscript. So when I use "we" in the book, it is with these outstanding students and their collective efforts in mind. Of course, all the lapses in logic and exposition are mine alone.

It is also important to acknowledge that the National Science Foundation, under award number 9732233 on "Determinants of State-Level Disaster Policy Change, Improvement, and Learning," supported the preliminary research that led to chapter 4.

Finally, as I was writing this book, my wife, Molly, and I experienced our own major events with the birth of our sons, Oskar and Isaak. Molly remains one of my best editors and collaborators, and not just of my academic work. The love and patience of my family sustained me as I wrote this book, and it is to my sons in particular that I dedicate this work, for I hope that our generation can learn from its mistakes and profit from its successes before we pass this world on to them.

one

theories and models of policy change and learning

This book is about the dynamics of policy change after sudden events known as focusing events. These sudden events include accidents, natural disasters, and deliberately caused catastrophes, such as terrorist attacks. The term *focusing event* entered widespread use among students of the agenda-setting phase of public policy in John Kingdon's seminal book, *Agendas, Alternatives, and Public Policies,* first published in 1984. In *After Disaster* (Birkland 1997a), I applied the idea of focusing events to disasters and accidents and found that disasters and accidents do indeed cause a discernible increase in the attention paid to a policy problem. This may seem obvious; it is intuitively sensible that people do not pay much attention to earthquakes or terrorist attacks until one actually happens. What was interesting about *After Disaster* was not merely the finding that disasters influence the agenda but the discovery that there is an interaction between the event, the nature of the event (human versus natural, for example), and the composition of the community of actors who address the policy issues or problems revealed by the disaster. In this interaction we can find rather different agenda-setting politics, ranging from the domain of hurricane policy, in which there are very few organized interests available to use the occurrence of a hurricane to effect

1

changes in hurricane policy, to the domain of nuclear power, which is so polarized that even a focusing event does not necessarily yield much movement in the positions of the contending parties.

This book expands on *After Disaster* by considering whether and to what extent policy change—not just agenda change—follows a disaster. I examine four policy domains: homeland security, aviation security, earthquakes, and hurricanes. The complexities and subtleties of the agenda-setting process that accompany focusing events are extended, if not magnified, by the process that determines whether policy will or should change after disasters. Whereas it is easy to give examples of policy change that accompanied and were seemingly caused by disasters, the processes of policy change are often subtle and complex, when change happens at all. One of the sources of complexity is the choice of theoretical framework for explaining change. In this book I explain how we can understand policy change as the result of learning processes in the policy process. I call policy change that can be plausibly linked to a particular event *event-related policy change*.

In *After Disaster* I defined a potential focusing event as "an event that is sudden, relatively rare, can be reasonably defined as harmful or revealing the possibility of greater potential future harms, inflicts harms or suggests potential harms that are or could be concentrated on a definable geographical or community of interest, and that is known to policymakers and the public virtually simultaneously" (Birkland 1997a). I defined *potential* focusing events in this way because there can be many events in a policy domain that do not become focusing events. An earthquake in a distant location may be an event in the seismological sense, and it may well be a harbinger of worse things to come in another locale, but an earthquake in the Aleutians will not have the same focal power for Americans that an earthquake in Los Angeles or Seattle will. Similarly, a hurricane that fails to strike populated areas is still a hurricane in the meteorological sense, but it is not a hurricane worth noting in human history.[1]

Crises, disasters, and catastrophes are three types of focusing events, as outlined in figure 1.1. In this book I adopt the distinction between crisis and disaster from Faulkner, who argues that crises are sometimes "induced by the actions or inactions of an organization," while disasters result from "induced natural phenomena or external human action" to which government or organizations can simply respond (Faulkner 2001, 137). Such responses range from immediate relief and recovery to efforts to mitigate the hazard should a future event take place. Whether or how crises emerge depends upon the way in which they are interpreted by relevant actors, which determines whether these events become policy issues.

Crises and disasters also differ in their scale, as shown in figure 1.1. Some crises are small scale, such as the flash flooding that, in the "Swiss Canyon incident," killed thrillseekers who went "canyoning," which involves hiking through whitewater in a narrow watercourse. This was a crisis for the company that led these tours and was certainly unfortunate, but it was not a disaster because of the relatively small scope of the event's effects and in particular because it was the result of the tour operator's carelessness. American crises include the *Exxon Valdez* oil spill, the Three Mile Island nuclear accident, the widespread food poisoning cases at the Jack in the Box restaurant chain in 1993, and the high-profile crash of ValuJet Flight 592 into the Florida Everglades in 1996 (Birkland and Nath 2000). In each case the problem was "induced by the actions or inactions of an organization."

Figure 1.1   Crises, Disasters, and Catastrophes

	Crises	Disasters	Catastrophes
↑ Scale or Magnitude of the Event	Chernobyl	September 11 attacks	Hurricane Katrina
	Exxon Valdez	Kobe earthquake	
			South Asia tsunami
	Tylenol poisoning	Pan Am 103	
	Swiss Canyon incident		
		Katherine flood (Australia)	

Source: Adapted from Faulkner (2001).

The flood in Katherine, Australia, a popular tourist area, falls into the disaster category because it was the result of forces beyond the effective control of the tourism industry in the region. Much larger disasters include the Chernobyl nuclear power plant accident and the Kobe earthquake of 1995; American disasters include Hurricane Andrew in 1992 and the Loma Prieta and Northridge earthquakes in 1989 and 1994, respectively, as well as the September 11 attacks. These events all involve natural disasters or terrorism, and although organizational failures clearly took place before and after these events, one cannot say that the actions of any one firm or organization caused or led directly to these disasters.

A further distinction arises from the idea that some disasters are *catastrophes*. Catastrophes are more profound than disasters because they affect a much broader area, render local and neighboring governments unable to respond because they, too, are affected, and therefore require considerable assistance from regional and national governments or from international or nongovernmental relief organizations (Quarantelli 2005). Recent catastrophes include the South Asia tsunami in 2004 and Hurricane Katrina and the major earthquake in Kashmir in 2005. Catastrophes are most likely to gain the greatest attention and therefore are the events most likely to trigger policy change.

The distinction between crisis, disaster, and catastrophe is useful, but the line between what constitutes a disaster and what constitutes a crisis is unclear. It will always be in the interest of some participants in policy debate to depict an event as a crisis triggered by willful action or gross human malfeasance (and therefore as the product of an organization or institution). Others may argue that the same event is a disaster or even a catastrophe over which the supposedly responsible organization had little or no control. Blame fixing is a key feature of causal stories; these stories are important both in agenda setting and in laying the groundwork for the selection of alternative policy directions (Stone 1989). Whether an event is a crisis, a disaster, or a catastrophe—and therefore whether it can effectively be blamed on some actor or organization—may be as much a social construction as an objective fact.

Regardless of its ultimate cause, a disaster has an influence on the broader social and political community. The larger the disaster in terms of lives lost, property damaged, and the physical area covered (that is, the more like a catastrophe the event is), the larger the potential influence on the political and policy world, all other things being equal. This follows Carter's definition of a disaster as "an event, natural or man-made, sudden or progressive, which impacts with such severity that the affected community has to respond by taking exceptional measures" (1991, xxiii). I depart from this definition by stipulating that most disasters are sudden. If a "disaster" builds gradually, it is more difficult to portray as a disaster because it is possible to detect the indicators of the developing problem, even if action is not immediately taken. Indeed, crises tend to build over time, whereas disasters strike suddenly. For example, the crash of ValuJet Flight 592 into the Everglades was the culmination of several organizational failures at the airline, not one sudden event. Nevertheless, the crash attracted attention and led to change. When an event is unanticipated (even if it is "inevitable" in the sense that we know it will happen eventually—for example, the major earthquake that we expect will strike Los Angeles, San Francisco, or Seattle someday), it affects both the way people react and the impact on the policy process. A sudden event means that the public and policymakers begin to scrutinize an issue nearly simultaneously. A disaster can often do in an instant what years of interest group activity, policy entrepreneurship, advocacy, lobbying, and research may not be able to do: elevate an issue on the agenda to a place where it is taken seriously in one or more policy domains.

A crisis can be internally generated or it can be the result of a disaster or some other undesirable event that strains an organization's adaptive capacity. Faulkner quotes Booth's definition of a crisis as "a situation faced by an individual, group or organization which they are unable to cope with by the use of normal routine procedures and in which stress is created by sudden change" (Booth 1993, 86). The entire field of crisis management is devoted to the development of nonnormal procedures to respond to nonroutine managerial problems. In other words, a disaster is what happens to individuals—those people in the path of a hurricane, for example—but the crisis is suffered by an organization, from the government broadly to individual agencies or groups. These groups must pay extraordinary attention to a crisis if they are to address it successfully. Crisis management becomes important because organizations (even ad hoc organizations that are spontaneously created in a disaster), not individual victims, are responsible for managing crises. Furthermore, what may be thought of as a "disaster" may not lead to a crisis for a particular organization if the organization is well prepared for potentially disastrous events. Earthquakes, hurricanes, and the like may always be stressful in some ways, but planning for disasters and taking steps to mitigate their effects may prevent them from rising to the level of crisis. Indeed, as we will see in this book, federal disaster relief policy is designed to routinize responses to predictable *types* of disasters. Natural disasters are predictable in the sense that we know that a big flood, earthquake, or hurricane will happen *somewhere, sometime* in the future. The goal of the government is to make responses to disasters routine, reduce strain on the disaster relief and management system, and therefore reduce the likelihood of organizational crisis in the national government. When responses become nonroutine, or when existing systems are overwhelmed in catastrophic disasters, such as after Hurricanes Andrew (1992) or Katrina (2005), crisis in the sense defined above is more likely.

A *policy domain* is the substantive subject of policy over which participants in policymaking compete and compromise (Burstein 1991; Knoke and Laumann 1982). Thus earthquakes are a policy domain, as are hurricanes (both part of a broader domain of natural disasters), aviation security, and homeland security. There is some overlap and nesting in these domains: Earthquakes and hurricanes are part of a broader natural hazards domain, and since September 11 natural disasters have become part of a broader "homeland security" or "public security" domain, although not entirely comfortably. Some participants in the earthquake and hurricane policy domains have little in common (for example, seismologists and meteorologists), whereas others (for example, disaster relief experts) are concerned with any natural disaster and therefore bridge the earthquake and hurricane domains. We will see the implications of this nesting and bridging in the case studies of natural disasters. The *policy community* consists of the individuals acting on behalf of groups that are actively involved in policymaking in a particular domain (Laumann and Knoke 1987).

Domains prone to disasters are policy domains that are the most sensitive to policy change in the wake of a disaster. These domains generally gain very little attention until a sudden event gives issues priority on the agenda. The domains that deal with earthquakes and hurricanes are almost by definition domains prone to disasters. People working in these domains seek to prepare for, respond to, and mitigate the effects of these disasters. Members of the aviation security domain are more concerned with *preventing* bombings, sabotage, and hijackings before these crimes happen and thus have a somewhat different job from those working in the natural disaster domains. Domains not prone to disasters include domains such as consumer product safety or most kinds of disease. In these domains problems become known slowly, as *indicators* of problems accumulate and become more evident. Harmful side effects of medicines or dangers of toys or automobiles do not become evident all at once; rather, problems arise nationally and worldwide as products are used, data accumulate, and analysts connect seemingly disparate events with common causes. And in many domains there are no single causes. In traffic safety, for example, nearly forty thousand fatalities a year can be laid to many causes, from drunk driving, to driver inattention, to vehicle design or highway design flaws, to simple bad luck. In the safety and disease domains, problems are often anticipated even if they are not successfully addressed. In 2005, for example, the problem of the H5N1 strain of bird influenza gained worldwide attention, and its transmission to humans in Turkey and Europe in early 2006 has increased concern about pandemic flu, and in particular about the possibility of its transmission from person to person rather than from birds to people. But a global flu pandemic is a different kind of disaster from the type described in this book because it can be anticipated before the pandemic occurs. Thus policy change can actually precede an event, and so the policy change dynamics are somewhat different from those I study here. One reason to study the process of learning from disasters is that efforts to learn and to change policy are likely to be accelerated in the wake of major events. At the same time, learning may be more difficult in domains prone to disaster because large events generally happen infrequently. Learning from such low-probability/high-consequence events is therefore likely to be challenging, particularly when policymakers are confronted with the urge to "do something," and when action, regardless of its value, may be more politically advantageous than more cautious and ultimately more effective deliberation.

Knowledge, Learning, and Policy Change

Policy scholars and political scientists have tended to view participation in policymaking and politics as a process in which power is wielded to promote an individual's or group's interests. Since the 1980s this primarily interest-driven notion of politics has given way to a more subtle understanding of politics and policymaking. As John Kingdon argues with his "streams metaphor" of agenda setting and alternative selection, this understanding relies on the substantive meaning of *ideas* in the policy process, and on the ability of actors in the policy process to prevail in competitions over ideas (1995). While power and interests are still important aspects of policymakers' behavior, the substance of what is being promoted and enshrined in policy is the *idea*.

Sabatier and Jenkins-Smith expand on the notion of ideas, noting that policies themselves are idea-driven belief systems:

> [P]olicies and programs incorporate implicit theories about how to achieve their objectives, and thus can be conceptualized in much the same way as belief systems. They involve value priorities, perceptions of important causal relationships, perceptions of world states (including the magnitude of the problem), perceptions of the efficacy of policy instruments, and so on. The ability to map beliefs and policies on the same "canvass" provides a vehicle for assessing the influence of various actors over time, particularly the role of technical information (belief) on policy change. (Sabatier and Jenkins-Smith 1993, 17)

The process by which participants use information and knowledge to develop, test, and refine their beliefs—the beliefs that motivate political action as well as the beliefs that find their way into policies—is the learning process. Busenberg defines a learning process as "the institutional arrangements and political events that shape individual learning" (2001, 173). This process is central to a theory of event-related policy change. Participants in policymaking may alter some of their beliefs as they learn more about the policy problem, the potential solutions to the problem, and the arguments they can make to advance their preferred policies. As these beliefs are altered, we can say that participants in policymaking are engaged in learning.

Why do individuals learn? Why do some theorists claim that organizations learn? Because human information-processing capacity is limited by our ability to gather and analyze all relevant information. People and the organizations in which they make decisions are *boundedly rational* (Simon 1957), which means that they seek to make rational decisions within the limits of information gathering and analysis capacity. Saying that humans are boundedly rational does not mean that people cannot improve their decisions, however. Rather, a model of decision making that rests on bounded rationality contains within it the idea that people have a problem-solving orientation; that is, people *want* to solve problems and make better decisions. It also contains the ability for people to make, correct, and learn from errors. People thereby develop "new understanding, and [adopt] new strategies in pursuit of their goals" (Busenberg 2001, 174, citing Ostrom 1999). In other words, social policy learning and political learning are occurring. The ultimate goal of social policy learning and political learning, however, is to actually effect change in some tangible way, and the most tangible evidence of policy change is new legislation and regulation.

To say that events lead to efforts to learn, that they contribute to the learning process, therefore assumes some degree of rationality among political actors and within political institutions. One might consider any system entirely dysfunctional if it failed to respond in some way to disasters or crises. At the other extreme would be fully rational behavior in which an event simply led to a set of calculations about what the "best" course of action would be based on at least two variables: the probability of the recurrence of the most recent disaster, and the consequences of the damage from any recurrent event. Indeed, these two variables are central to our discussion of what students of disasters and catastrophes call "low-probability/high-consequence events." Both must be taken seriously: One need not be too concerned about an event that has few if any consequences, whether it happens daily or once in a thousand years. Rainstorms happen all the time, but they are generally inconsequential from a flood policy perspective. Nevertheless, if a potential event is catastrophic, even the *possibility* of its return must be taken seriously (Clarke 2005a); probability alone is insufficient for making policy about potentially catastrophic events.

Humans and their institutions behave in ways that are boundedly rational, then, but also adaptive. Bryan Jones, in *Politics and the Architecture of Choice,* sought to better understand "more careful comparisons of adaptive behavior and its failure in particular situations" (Jones 2001, xi). Jones employs a rich literature in the social and behavioral sciences to argue that humans and our institutions have important limits, are boundedly rational, and are adaptive within limits.

Jones outlines the basic argument of his book as follows:

> (1) Human behavior is mostly adaptive and goal-oriented. (2) Because of biological limits on cognitive capacities, however, humans are disproportionate information processors. They tend to react to new information by neglect or overestimation. (3) The formal organizations created by humans aid in adaptation by overcoming inherited limitations in adaptive abilities. (4) Nevertheless, some of our limitations in adaptability will show through in even the most rational of institutions. (5) As a consequence, these institutions will not react proportionately to incoming information, and outputs from the most rational of institutions will be disjointed and episodic. (Jones 2001, 25)

People are goal oriented and want to solve problems. In the case of focusing events, there is ample evidence, at least in the agenda-setting literature, that a sudden event will lead to a disproportionate amount of attention to the issues revealed by the most recent disaster. This is because the fact that an event has occurred generally does not change the overall risk of any future event happening; rather, what has changed is the level of interest in, attention to, and perhaps appreciation of the possibility of an event's recurrence. In other words, this disproportionate increase in attention to and concern about an issue is the complement to the disproportionate lack of concern and attention to the problem before the focusing event.

This increased attention does not necessarily mean that learning will occur, however. Increased attention alone is insufficient evidence of any sort of learning. Rather, we should be able to link attention to actual policy change. Are the organizations in policy communities able and prepared to learn from disasters, and to what extent? This question is taken up in the case studies addressed in the following chapters. In particular, those chapters look for evidence that some sort of learning process led to policy change.

We can base our understanding of policy change and learning on features of human behavior as reflected in organizations and institutions. The first of these features is "intended rationality." People seek to be as rational as possible; social scientists often find the many ways in which people deviate from this intended rationality particularly interesting and worthy of study (Jones 2001, 54). Second, in some cases people are prepared to take in new information and deliberate on their responses to it, while in other cases people must react very quickly in the face of new information. Neither model of reaction to information is optimal in all cases, nor can an individual react quickly and deliberatively at the same time. Jones calls this tension the "preparation-deliberation tradeoff." The decision how to respond to some crises and disasters requires a degree of deliberation, but if existing rules and procedures are close at hand, they may well be used even if they are almost immediately found wanting. Available tools may also be pressed into service because of extreme pressures to act quickly in crises and disasters. The continued failure of existing tools and processes in the face of a disaster may provide a powerful impetus for learning and policy change after a disaster.

Different Types of Learning

From a normative perspective, it is evident that people *should* learn from disasters. Newspapers and journals of all stripes have discussed the "lessons of 9/11" or "the lessons of Hurricane Katrina" as if we will inevitably—and almost automatically—learn from these events. This is not necessarily the case. Part of the difficulty in explaining how we learn or fail to learn from disasters lies in the difficulty of developing a model of learning.

Researchers must make clear at the outset whether their model of learning allows nonhuman entities such as institutions or organizations to "learn." Most students of the policy process assume that individuals—agency heads, interest group leaders, academics, journalists, and so on—are the key objects of learning in the policy process (Busenberg 2001; Levy 1994; May 1992; Sabatier 1987, 1991; Sabatier and Jenkins-Smith 1993). Indeed, Sabatier (1987) argues that learning at the level of groups and organizations is largely "metaphorical," because organizations do not have the cognitive capacity to "learn." I adopt Sabatier's assumption that individuals learn. However, as noted above, we can also stipulate that participants in policymaking know of their cognitive and information-processing limits; they therefore create organizations to capitalize on the ability of people to work together to seek solutions while seeking to overcome the limitations of *individual* decision making (Jones 2001).

Once we address the question of who learns, we must address the question of *what* is learned. This is not as straightforward as one might suppose. Scholars who have considered the question of learning have outlined different theories of both the process of learning and the object of learning, as summarized in table 1.1. Bennett and Howlett (1992) identify four prominent students of learning in the policy process: Hugh Heclo, Peter Hall, Lloyd Etheredge, and Paul Sabatier. Hugh Heclo's seminal 1974 study suggested that "political learning" is "a governmental response to some kind of social or environmental stimulus" (Bennett and Howlett 1992, 277). This is an attractive way of thinking about learning from disasters and other focusing events, for the stimulus for learning—the event—is obvious and its effects can to some extent be separated from the "background noise" of normal policymaking.

Peter Hall (1993), however, describes what he calls "social learning" as more measured and deliberate than Heclo's political learning. "As [Hall] puts it, learning is a 'deliberate attempt to adjust the goals or techniques of policy in the light of the consequences of past policy and new information so as to better attain the ultimate objects of governance'" (Bennett and Howlett 1992, 277, quoting Hall 1988). Bennett and Howlett note that Heclo's notion of responding to an external stimulus and the "deliberate" attempt

Table 1.1 Types of Learning, Who Learns, and What Is Learned

Learning Type	Who Learns	Learns What	To What Effect
Government learning	State officials	Process related	Organizational change (Etheredge)
Lesson drawing	Policy networks	Instruments	Program change (Rose, some Heclo)
Social learning	Policy communities	Ideas (Sabatier)	Paradigm shift (Hall, some Heclo)
Political learning	Political actors	Strategies	Improved arguments for particular policies (May)

Source: Adapted from Bennett and Howlett (1992), 289, fig. 1.

to adjust goals or policy tools may be two ways of describing the same sort of stimulus–response mechanism that characterizes much of the policy process. The difference, if there is one, is that Heclo suggests that learning is a less conscious activity, while Hall argues that learning is a conscious action explicitly linked to the motivation for policy change.

Etheredge (1985) first posed the question "can governments learn?" and his "government learning" is more closely associated with organizational theory than the other categories are. "Although themselves divided in terms of a precise definition of learning, organizational theorists share notions of organizational adaptation and behavior change due to knowledge accumulation and value-change within institutions and their members. Etheredge suggests these concepts apply equally to public orga-nizations as to private firms" (Bennett and Howlett 1992, 277, internal citations omitted). This is a useful application of orga-nizational theory to the public policy process, but I will not rely heavily on this conception of learning, both because it fails to specify precisely what learning is and because Etheredge focuses on individual organizations rather than on the broader range of actors in the policy community.

At the heart of Sabatier's Advocacy Coalition Framework (ACF) is "policy-oriented learning," which is learning about "relatively en-during alterations of thought or behavioral intentions that result from experience and are concerned with the attainment or revi-sion of the precepts of one's belief system" (Sabatier 1987, 672). As noted above, belief systems are important in Sabatier's frame-work. This framework argues that while policy-oriented learning is an important aspect of policy change and can often alter periph-eral features of a coalition's belief system, changes in the core aspects of a policy are usually the result of perturbations in non-cognitive factors external to the subsystem, such as macroeco-nomic conditions or the rise of a new systemic governing coalition (Sabatier 1988, 134).

In essence, learning is a day-to-day activity, but it does not often change the core of an individual's or interest group's belief system. Larger systemic shocks—perhaps larger than just a focusing event by itself—are required, such as the political realignments in the United States that preceded the Civil War, which led to the demise of the Whig Party, or the Great Depression, which created a New Deal coalition in the Democratic Party that lasted nearly fifty years. These major shifts are not the result of one event but are often driven by a combination of related events. In the case of the New Deal, Franklin Roosevelt was required to react quickly to problems that resulted from the crash of the stock market, the collapse of the world trading system under crushing tariffs, the liquidity crisis of the early 1930s, and the related insolvency of many banks. Although the causes of these events are complex and hard to sort into neat categories, we can argue that the responses to these crises led to learning based on both experience and ongoing policy experimentation. Indeed, one of Roosevelt's most famous statements, made in response to demands that the government address the Depression, is this: "The country needs and, unless I mistake its temper, the country demands *bold, persistent experimentation.* It is common sense to take a method and try it; if it fails, admit it frankly and try another. But above all, try something" (emphasis added).[2]

Perhaps the most obvious form of learning is lesson drawing (Rose 1993). This is different from experimentation. Lesson drawing involves scanning nearby jurisdictions or more distant places for policy ideas that can be applied to local situations; it is both stimulus driven and *externally* focused, but the mechanisms for learning—and the reasons for mere mimicking or copying—are not well defined. While lesson drawing may be important, particularly in federal systems, where subnational governments draw lessons from other governments' experiences, lesson drawing is less a theoretical framework than a description of how learning proceeds. It relates directly to what Peter May (1992) calls instrumental policy learning, described in the next section.

In the end, no one type of learning can account for the full range of learning that can occur after a disaster. May's depiction of learning from policy failure incorporates the strongest features of these learning types and provides a bridge between learning, policy failure, and disasters.

Policy Failure and Learning

In *After Disaster* I argued that focusing events get so much attention because they provide evidence of policy failure. May links policy failure to learning and in particular provides guidance as to what would serve as evidence of learning. This is very important: May's 1992 article is one of the few works on this subject that considers the empirical implications of studying learning. May also draws upon the literature reviewed above to generate his theory of failure-inspired learning. He argues that policy failure inspires three different kinds of learning: instrumental policy learning, social policy learning, and political learning.

Instrumental policy learning is learning about the "viability of policy interventions or implementation designs." This learning centers on implementation tools and techniques.[3] While this appears to be similar to lesson drawing, it differs in that it can involve indirect experience with the performance of policy instruments but also direct experience with policy instruments. When we analyze feedback from implementation and make changes in design that improve performance, we have prima facie evidence that learning has happened. Instrumental policy learning is central to this study because it is relatively easy to demonstrate the existence of policy change by pointing to legislation or regulation; one can then trace the ideas that fed into policy change in media reports, records of debates, congressional hearings, or public comments on proposed regulation.

Social policy learning involves learning about the "social construction of a policy or program." This learning goes beyond simple adjustments in program management to the heart of the problem itself, including attitudes toward program goals and the nature and appropriateness of government action. If applied successfully, social policy learning can result in better understanding of the underlying causal theory of a public problem, leading to better policy responses. Social policy learning involves the interplay of ideas about how problems come about and how they can be solved, and is much more likely to engage ideology and belief systems than are more practical aspects of instrumental learning. This distinction is not a precise one, however; the choice of policy tools is also influenced greatly by beliefs about what will work and what is desirable from managerial and ideological perspectives.

Political learning is considerably different from instrumental and social learning. Political learning consists of learning about "strategy for advocating a given policy idea or problem," leading potentially to "more sophisticated advocacy of a policy idea or problem" (May 1992, 339). Political learning occurs when advocates and opponents of policy change alter their political and rhetorical strategies and tactics to conform to new information that has entered the political system.

In the ideal case, learning reflects the accumulation and application of knowledge and leads to better policies. But policymakers and their supporters may support policy change that is not objectively related to the actual problems revealed by a given event. May calls mimicking or copying policy without assessment or analysis "superstitious instrumental learning." Copying or mimicking can lead to positive policy outcomes by accident rather than by design. Stakeholders may believe that a policy is an improvement or at least is not harmful if the near-term outcomes are no worse, and perhaps better, than the outcomes of the policies that were replaced.

A Model of Event-Related Policy Change

Thomas Dye argues that "a model is merely an abstraction or representation of political life" (1992, 44). Good models seek to order and simplify reality, identify what is significant about a system, and square it with reality to the extent that this is possible. Models should communicate meaningful information about the policy process, including direct inquiry and research, and suggest explanations for public policy. On this last point, Dye argues that models "should *suggest* hypotheses about the causes and consequences of public policy" (45). Another useful feature of a model is parsimony both in its form and in the phenomenon it is attempting to describe; a model should be no more complex than it has to be to explain a given event.

The model outlined in figure 1.2 seeks to fulfill these criteria. In particular it helps us to generate propositions about what we might see in the policy process in domains prone to disaster. These propositions would suggest the data needed to understand a given event.

The first proposition is that most if not all participants in a policy domain want to address or solve the problems revealed by a focusing event, but that the proposed solutions are likely to

Figure 1.2 A Model of Event-Related Policy Learning

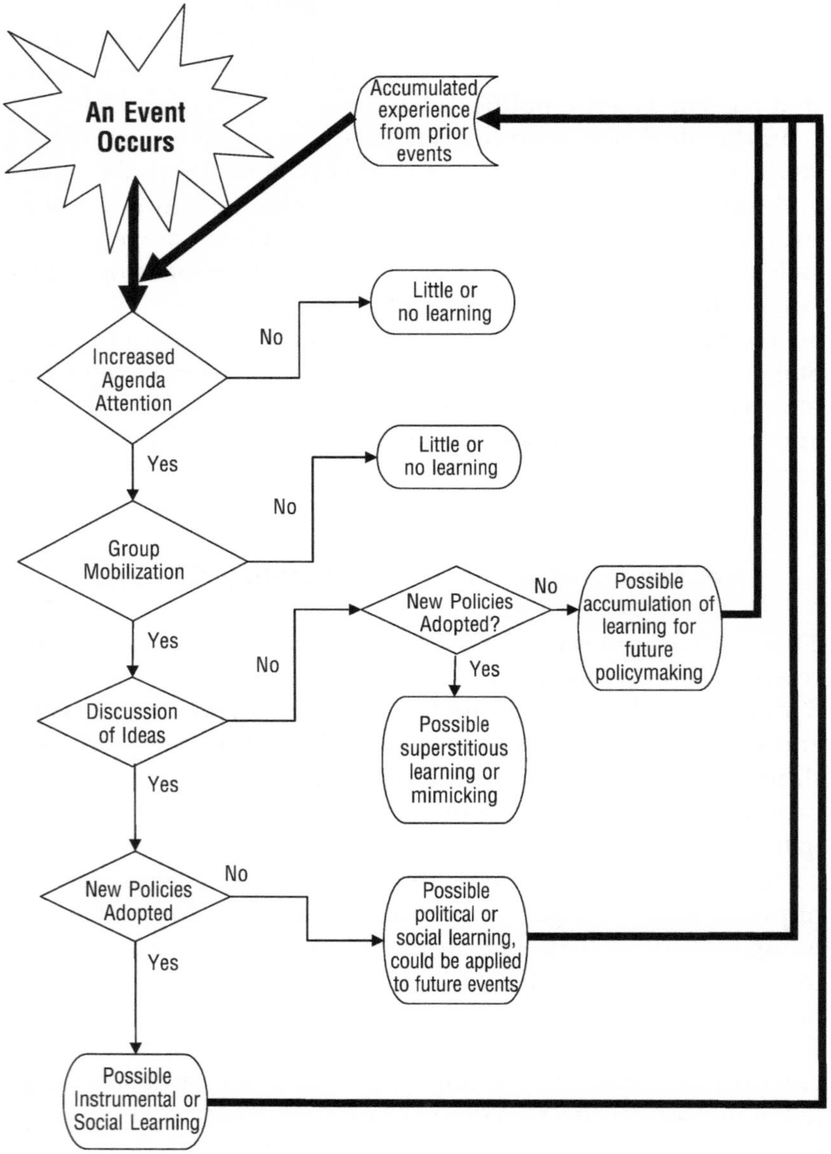

vary with the interests and motivations of these participants. This reflects the idea that nearly all participants in a domain are goal oriented, as suggested by Jones (2001) and as implied by the literature on learning. No legitimate actor in any policy domain wants to see planes hijacked or people displaced by natural disasters. But the policy instruments through which problems will be prevented or mitigated will differ from participant to participant in the policy process because the depiction of *how* problems come to be, and therefore how they are solved, will be different depending on each participant's ideological and organizational commitments.

The second proposition is that a few events will gain the most attention. The distribution of damage and deaths in disasters and accidents is not statistically normal; rather, the distribution of focusing events has a long "tail," where a large number of relatively small events garner little attention, and a few big events garner a great deal. For example, many tropical storms or hurricanes can strike the eastern United States during hurricane season, but only the very largest storms, on the scale of Hurricanes Katrina or Andrew, get serious attention and have the greatest potential influence on learning. Smaller incidents do not get attention because they are often successfully addressed by existing organizations and policies; Hurricane Katrina got more attention than did all four of the hurricanes that struck Florida in 2004 because the response to the Florida hurricanes was generally perceived as adequate, and because no individual storm was catastrophic, whereas Katrina was a catastrophe that overwhelmed the national emergency management system.

The third proposition is that group mobilization is linked in time to a particular focusing event. In particular, the activities of groups—or the representatives of such groups—will become more evident in news accounts of the issue. In congressional hearings, particular groups' representatives will be heard from more often. In the media and in the legislative branch, these actors' activities will be clearly linked to an event.

The fourth proposition is that group mobilization will be accompanied by an increase in discussion of policy ideas. This will include theories about the causes of and potential solutions to the problem and as such are primarily social and instrumental policy learning matters. Evidence of political learning may also be present, but such evidence may be less apparent, given that this learning happens for the most part internally, within organizations in the policy domain or advocacy coalitions. In any case, policy learning is much less likely without the mobilization of ideas, and ideas are unlikely to come to the fore without some sort of group mobilization.

Thus the fifth proposition is that there is a relationship between ideas and policy change. In particular, change is more likely when ideas become more prominent after events than when they do not. Policy change can occur without ideas, but such policy change is not typically the result of careful debate and therefore does not result from learning; instead it is mimicking or copying without learning (May 1992). Table 1.2 shows the types of evidence one would use to illustrate learning as conceptualized in these propositions.

The sixth proposition is that it is possible for learning to decay over time. While policy change may result from an event, the time that intervenes between one focusing event and another and the demands placed on policymakers in that intervening period may cause participants in the policy process to "forget" the lessons they learned. In this study I am more concerned with event-related policy change and learning than I am with the long-term decay, if any, of the lessons of a given event.

As I finished writing this book in late 2005, Hurricane Katrina struck the Gulf Coast of the United States, resulting in what appears to be the largest natural disaster in terms of monetary damage in American history. The effects of Hurricane Katrina, and the apparently fumbled federal, state, and local response to the event, suggest that the putative lessons of Hurricane Andrew were not fully learned, were forgotten over time, or were influenced by the interaction between the natural hazards and the "homeland security" domains. Kingdon calls these interactions between policy domains "spillovers," and such spillovers can theoretically reinforce or retard learning. I will show that the focus on homeland security had a corrosive influence on the nation's preparedness for natural disasters. I address this problem of decay in more fully in chapter 5, where I discuss the implications of event-related policy change for policy implementation.

Table 1.2   Typical Evidence of Learning in the Policy Process

Organization or Institution	*Evidence of Learning*
News media	Stories about the problem Changes in the nature of news coverage (people quoted, substance of news coverage)
Interest groups	Change in appearances at congressional hearings Increased attention from news media (generated by the group)
Congress	Legislative change Change in the substance of debate Change in the topic areas of hearings
Regulatory and implementing agencies	Issuance of new and proposed regulations Change in the nature and substance of the regulations being issued Change in procedures and in the interpretation and implementation of statutes and regulations.

Figure 1.2 depicts what I call event-related learning. In this model, if actions occur at various points after a focusing event occurs, learning becomes more likely, as does policy change as a result of this learning. This model also suggests that learning without policy change may occur after one event, or that policy change may result from mimicking or "superstitious" learning. This kind of learning is the result of pressure to "do something" after an event without any careful analysis. Whether learning occurred is a qualitative judgment that must be made within the context of each case study. Finally, the model acknowledges that not every event will lead to policy change but that events may contribute to a base of experience that may promote learning from subsequent events as knowledge accumulates, as depicted by the feedback arrow.

I adopt Busenberg's definition of learning as "a process in which individuals apply new information and ideas to policy decisions." I modify this definition slightly, however, and define learning as a process in which individuals apply new information and ideas, or information and ideas elevated on the agenda by a recent event, to policy decisions. This amendment takes into account the ebb and flow of ideas on the agenda and the accumulation of ideas over time, even as those ideas are not uniformly translated into policy. For example, the risk of catastrophic terrorist attacks on the United States was probably about the same on September 12, 2001, as it was on September 10, but the September 11 attacks caused the public and elites to be much more attentive to the terrorism problem. A focusing event brings information to the attention of a broader range of people than normally consider the issues.

I do not claim to be able to measure "learning" directly at the individual level on the basis of behavioral-scientific notions of learning or improvement in cognitive skills. Rather, I focus on the apparent lessons of these events and ask whether it appears that the clear lessons of these events have been learned, as reflected in the policymaking process. In particular, we can say that there is prima facie evidence of learning if policy changes in a way that is reasonably likely to mitigate the problem revealed by the focusing event. This operationalization of learning cedes a great deal of judgment to the researcher making the claim that learning has occurred. The case studies in the chapters that follow will show, however, that empirical and narrative analyses can provide a strong base for learning or the lack thereof.

In the beginning of the process, an event happens. The first crucial step is for the event to gain attention. If it fails to gain much attention, it is unlikely to result in much group and policymaker mobilization. Events that fall into the low-attention category generally include events that do relatively little damage, appear to be unthreatening, or appear to be well contained within existing policies and require little or no action on anyone's part. The several cockpit intrusions that occurred in commercial airliners before September 11 are examples of such events; drunk or otherwise disorderly passengers perpetrated most such intrusions. The system then in place, which required that the cockpit door be closed and rather weakly locked, was deemed able to cope with the occasional inconvenience of an intrusion. The threats contemplated before September 11 were not considered sufficient to require a more secure cockpit. In other words, the existing system treated the possibility of a fatal cockpit intrusion as very remote.[4] Even when intrusions received much attention, they failed to cause groups and policymakers to move toward understanding whether policy failure had occurred and whether something should be done about it. The failure to mobilize stymies learning because learning requires competition between advocacy coalitions, as each side tries to marshal evidence and knowledge about the policy process and about political tactics to advance its goals. By group mobilization, however, I do not mean broad-based citizens' groups or social movements but the relatively small groups of professionals, experts, and advocates that are mostly likely to be energized by an event.

If there is discernible group mobilization after a focusing event, we should expect to see a discussion of ideas in various forums—that is, an exchange of opinions, beliefs, and theories about why the event happened and whether existing policy can address the problems revealed by the event. If a policy is shown to have failed, the discussion will include policies that seek to remedy the failure and prevent recurrence. It is at this stage that we may see considerable evidence of learning. If there is change without such a discussion, it is possible that mimicking or superstitious learning is at work. If, by contrast, we can draw a link between ideas, an event, and increased attention to ideas and new policies, then we have strong evidence of instrumental policy learning, and possibly also some evidence of social policy learning and political learning.

Learning and Lessons in This Study

Evidence of political, social policy, and instrumental learning varies in both type and ease of identification. May notes that it is very difficult to find definitive evidence of political learning in a domain because secondary sources "rarely provide detail about the relevant policy elite's causal reasoning about a policy problem or solution, often lack explanations for the choice of particular policy objectives or instruments, and are sketchy about different advocates' political strategies" (1992, 349). Prima facie indicators of social learning involve "policy redefinition entailing changes in policy goals or scope—e.g., policy direction, target groups, rights bestowed by the policy" (336).

As noted above, it is easiest to provide prima facie evidence of instrumental learning because a great deal of substantive legislation will often follow a focusing event. The substance of that legislation will often reveal the extent to which instrumental learning has occurred. The traces left by the legislative process—for example, in legislation that was introduced but failed to pass, media coverage, congressional testimony, and the like—provide at least indirect evidence of learning after a disaster, while an actual change in the law is obviously the most direct and important evidence.

I have adopted this somewhat stringent standard of evidence of learning because it is hard to measure learning outcomes without concrete evidence of change. Of course, the passage of legislation or enactment of a new regulation is not necessary to show that some sort of learning is likely to have occurred. As Kingdon notes, a focusing event, or anything else that moves the key streams together, merely opens a window of opportunity for change, without any guarantee of change itself. Thus I analyze both legislation that has passed into law and legislation that has not.

Methods

To assess these propositions requires the collection of data on key aspects of the policy process, as outlined in table 1.2.

Policy change can be defined broadly or narrowly. The most palpable form of policy change involves constitutional amendments or the enactment of major legislation. Lesser forms of change include modifications in regulations or standard operating procedures and transformations in the behavior of "street-level bureaucrats" (Lipsky 1978). In each of these instances policy change is detectable to some degree, but the mechanism by which this change occurs is often unspecified.

In this book I use proposed and enacted legislation and regulations as evidence of policy change, or movement in the direction of policy change, as reflections that some sort of learning may have occurred. Legislation and regulations are tangible evidence of learning outcomes, and we can assume that they are likely to be "reasonably enduring."

An important source of data for my case studies is the testimony of witnesses who appeared before congressional hearings. Congress is a good institutional venue to study, as its activities are consistently well documented through transcripts of testimony at hearings, committee reports, bills, and the like. Members of Congress, motivated by the desire to make good policy or by pressure from their constituents, are likely to react to focusing events. Specifically, congressional testimony is an appropriate indicator of group activity because it is among the most popular lobbying techniques employed by interest groups (Davidson and Oleszek 1994, 298). Because Congress keeps such copious records, congressional hearings provide a good record of what groups were most active in the policy domain, at least as far as Congress is concerned.

I found hearings using the Congressional Information Service index via the LexisNexis online database. This database allows researchers to isolate hearings on particular topics using a keyword search. This method is similar to that used by Baumgartner and Jones (1993), but as in *After Disaster* my unit of analysis is the individual witness before each hearing. I did not code appropriations hearings because they tend to cover routine budget matters and hear from a very limited range of witnesses compared with other legislative and oversight hearings. Once I had isolated hearings, I included them in a database listing each hearing and witness. I coded witnesses' testimony for group affiliation, the main subject of their testimony, and whether the testimony was related to a particular event. I used a very conservative method to code the last variable—the witness needed to mention the event directly in his or her testimony. I then categorized the witness's group affiliations by group type (industry, government, interest group, and so on) to understand how broad categories of groups behaved in the wake of focusing events.

Congressional testimony does have some shortcomings as a measure of an issue's importance. The partisan balance of

Congress or a committee chair's political preferences can influence the nature and number of witnesses. Furthermore, Congress is not the only arena of group activity or conflict. Mass protests and media pressure are two other methods of influencing policy. Still, focusing events can reasonably be expected to generate congressional testimony from groups that seek change as a result of the event. The event may be of such magnitude that it could be politically dangerous for a committee chair (and his or her allies outside Congress) to exclude opposing witnesses from hearings. Indeed, from the perspective of more powerful groups, it may be strategically wise to let such opponents vent their frustration at hearings, so as to prevent it from boiling over into other forms of political expression that could exert real pressure for policy change (Molotch 1970).

Another issue in the use of congressional testimony is the question of partisan control of the legislative branch and its concomitant influence on which witnesses are allowed to testify. But the issues studied here are not obviously partisan; we cannot say that aviation security is a liberal or conservative issue, or a Democratic or Republican issue, even if proposed policy tools may be more closely associated with a particular party or ideology. To the extent that partisanship matters, it can reasonably be assumed to be part of the "error term" of any model of focusing event dynamics. Of course, we can say that the potential solutions to the problem will reflect partisan preferences, but it is unlikely that a large focusing event will be ignored. Focusing events are of great interest to the news media and elite actors, and Congress, regardless of the party in power, will ignore such events at its peril. Data from floor debates that reflect the attitudes of rank-and-file members of Congress were gathered from the *Congressional Record* via the Library of Congress's Thomas search engine (http://thomas.loc.gov). Legislation was gathered from the same source.

News coverage of these focusing events, gathered to provide a sense of the broader public agenda, was generally collected from the *New York Times* via LexisNexis. I use the *New York Times* as a measure of the public agenda for substantive and practical reasons. The *Times* is readily accessible and searchable electronically, which makes it a particularly useful source, but it is also widely viewed as the national "paper of record," one that "aspire[s] to high journalistic standards" (Lawrence 2000a, 11) and thus epitomizes professionalism and journalistic excellence. For these reasons the *Times* has remarkable power in setting the agenda for other media outlets, such as the network news broadcasts (Auletta 2005).[5]

In the case studies that follow, the data collected are not fully parallel. Rather, I seek to use these data, and data from other sources as deemed necessary (such as local news coverage of disasters, employed in chapter 2) to illustrate what I see as the history of ideas and learning in a particular policy domain.

The Case Studies

Many policy domains are prone to disasters. A wide range of natural disasters, from the generally inconvenient, such as blizzards, to the potentially catastrophic, such as earthquakes and hurricanes, have the potential to change perceptions of problems and thus policy. Accidents that are a consequence of modern technology can also lead to policy change, but these accidents have the added dimension of being caused by—or at least blamed on— human error. The politics of policymaking after such events is likely to be different in analytically important ways, and it is worthwhile to consider both kinds of disasters, natural and "humanly caused."

Because of the breadth of these two categories, I focus on four types of disaster: domestic terrorist attacks (specifically the September 11 attacks), earthquakes and hurricanes (which I consider in one chapter because of some important similarities and contrasts), and aviation security breaches with fatal outcomes. The particular events of interest occurred in the United States. I study domestic events because they have the most direct and discernible effects on national policymaking. More details about each policy domain are provided in the following chapters, but we can briefly consider whether there are likely to be learning opportunities in these policy domains.

The first case study in this book is the September 11 terrorist attacks. One reason to study this case is that this was perhaps the most widely reported one-day catastrophe in world history. Because global communication is nearly instantaneous, a much larger proportion of the world's population learned of this event within minutes or hours after the first plane struck the World Trade Center than has ever learned of a similar event so quickly. From a learning perspective, the September 11 attacks are important because they triggered the sweeping reexamination of a wide range of issues related to what has come to be known as "homeland security." The key question I consider in the case study is whether and to what extent the attacks led to policy change as a result of learning, or whether change occurred without learning. The analysis is painted with a broad brush because the September 11 attacks had a profound influence on a wide range of policy issues.

The second case study is a more intensive examination of a key feature of the September 11 attacks: the failure of the aviation security system to prevent hijackings. The problems of the aviation security system were not unknown before September 11. At least once a week since 1995 the aviation industry confronted some breach or attempted breach of the passenger screening system. Passengers, most often inadvertently, were caught attempting to carry prohibited items such as knives, chemicals, and occasionally guns onto aircraft. But only two major security incidents gained widespread public attention and influenced policy before September 11, 2001. The first of these was the bombing of Pan Am Flight 103 over Scotland in 1988. The second, the destruction of TWA Flight 800 off Long Island, New York, in 1996, was initially attributed to a terrorist bombing because the airplane exploded in a manner eerily similar to that of Pan Am 103. Mechanical failure was eventually isolated as the cause, and the FAA recently has begun to require that aircraft be fitted with devices that will reduce the possibility of fuel tank explosions.

Then came the terrorist attacks of September 11, 2001, which could be disaggregated into four, or even nineteen, separate breaches that allowed nineteen terrorists to hijack four commercial airliners in domestic service. Two planes were crashed into the World Trade Center in New York, destroying it, one crashed into the Pentagon, severely damaging it, and one crashed into a field near Shanksburg, Pennsylvania, the result either of a passenger uprising or of confusion in the cockpit.

We can therefore say with some confidence that across the three policy domains there are at least nine opportunities for learning, although the TWA crash is a bit of an anomaly, since it was not caused by a terrorist attack. Yet this crash may be the most fascinating single case, because it led initially to the conclusion that aviation security required attention. The mounting evidence that the plane was lost because of mechanical failure may have short-circuited efforts to pass legislation or regulations designed to prevent terrorist attacks on aviation; instead, the focus was on aviation *safety* rather than security.

The third case study considers whether and to what extent learning occurs after earthquakes and hurricanes. It is not surprising that there are several opportunities for policy learning in both the earthquake and hurricane domains. Between 1988 and 2004 there were at least three major hurricanes that were widely publicized and led to some attention to the problem: Hugo in 1989, Andrew in 1992, and Floyd in 1999. During the same period, there were two very damaging earthquakes—the 1989 Loma Prieta and 1994 Northridge earthquakes—and one somewhat less damaging earthquake, the Nisqually. The Nisqually earthquake struck near Olympia, Washington, in early 2001, causing mainly superficial damage in the Seattle area and substantial structural damage to structures and buildings in Olympia.

Conclusions

Postdisaster policy learning is more than simply a matter of agenda setting. Whether it seeks something more tangible than "greater attention" to a problem is the question of interest here. From a normative perspective, citizens expect government and other officials to learn from disasters and to prevent repeat disasters, or at least to prevent repeat mistakes in the response to disasters. Failure to learn from experience is particularly embarrassing to members of government if the mistakes of the past are repeated. If the political system and broader social systems fail to learn from these events, the public can plausibly claim that these systems are dysfunctional. There is thus a considerable incentive to learn. At the same time, policymakers must calculate the costs of learning against the likelihood that an event will recur on their watch. If another catastrophic hurricane, earthquake, or terrorist attack is not expected to happen during a policymaker's tenure, the benefits that would accrue from the considerable efforts involving in learning and improving policy performance will not benefit the policymaker in the near term. Furthermore, the costs of change can be considerable if they mobilize opposition to change.

The chapters that follow explore whether and to what extent the increased attention that follows disasters leads policymakers to define problems and adopt new policies to address them. The concluding chapter assesses the model of event-centered policy change introduced in this chapter and considers reasons why learning happens or fails to happen after major disasters. It also looks at how learning fades over time, as other issues clamor for attention and policymakers forget the lessons of the past.

two

september 11, learning, and policy change

One would presume that an event as well documented as the terrorist attacks of September 11, 2001, constituted a classic focusing event: The event was rare—in fact, almost unprecedented—deadly, and caught the government and the public by surprise. The changes that followed the September 11 attacks have created a sprawling policy domain, "homeland security," that evolved from older notions of counterterrorism, national security, and emergency management.

Even the casual observer of public policy must know that September 11 did "change things": The simple acts of boarding a commercial airliner or crossing the U.S.–Canadian border have changed considerably since September 11, 2001. A new agency, the Department of Homeland Security, was created, although the term "new" is certainly contestable, considering that the DHS brought together at least twenty-two existing agencies and functions into one large and, many claim, unwieldy bureaucracy.

But can these policy changes be attributed to some sort of learning process? Recall Busenberg's definition of learning as "a process in which individuals apply *new information and ideas* to policy decisions" (emphasis added), and my expansion of this definition to include the proposition that learning is cumulative and experience amassed over time. To what extent did the September 11 attacks inject new information and ideas into an existing "policy stream"?

One must approach this question with care and indeed with some skepticism, given how loosely the term "the lessons of September 11" has been bandied about in the media and in government circles. Sociologist Lee Clarke has argued forcefully that very little learning has happened as a result of the September 11 attacks, because we already knew about our vulnerability to terrorist attack *before* September 11, 2001. "The 'lessons learned from 9.11' come to sound homiletic, too easy, even vacuous," Clarke writes. But there *are* some things, he says, "that we *should have* learned by now," namely,

- People are resilient in the face of catastrophe;
- People hardly ever panic in disasters;
- Americans are despised in many parts of the world;
- We won't be safe from terrorism by chest-thumping and bombing people;
- Our airports are vulnerable;
- Our critical infrastructure is vulnerable. (Clarke 2003, 3)

Clarke continues, "All of those things were known well before 9.11 by academics who know about terrorism and disasters. That's another reason that talk about 'lessons learned' is often so much hot air. The lessons are already there but elites have to pay attention if they are to matter." This is a crucial point. The policy changes that occurred after September 11 were based on information that was well known before the event, not just to academics but to experts in civilian agencies, the military, the private sector (such as the airlines), law enforcement—indeed, in a wide range of organizations, both public and private. Information and ideas accumulate. Ideas do not arise out of whole cloth after every event; they are the products of a much longer-term process.

There is no question that much of what we know about disaster preparedness and response predates September 11, 2001. Indeed, I explore in chapter 5 how it is that learning in the homeland security domain can coincide with "unlearning" the lessons amassed over time in emergency management policy. This is because the homeland security and emergency management domains overlap but are not the same. I disagree with Clarke on at least one point, however, because my research shows that policymakers have learned about homeland security issues, and they are the agents of learning with whom I am most concerned. In particular, the September 11 attacks provided information that seemed new to many of the most visible participants in post–September 11 policymaking. Applying Kingdon's streams metaphor, the September 11 attacks simply focused attention on a previously existing problem stream.

September 11 opened a rather large window of opportunity for policy change and learning because it changed both mass and elite perceptions of the risk or likelihood of terrorist attacks. The September 11 attacks also created a much broader sense that current policy tools were not working or, more to the point, were insufficient, given the newly revealed nature of the international terrorist threat. Indeed, the attacks forced a change in the social construction of the problem of terrorism, as it was transformed from a problem of law enforcement and intelligence gathering to one best met through affirmative and even aggressive military, economic, and diplomatic efforts. In essence, starting in the 1990s, terrorism shifted from a problem of criminal justice to a problem of national security. While this shift was occurring in elite circles to some extent before September 11, "national security" is now the dominant construction of terrorism in American policy, and the primary proponents of this position claim that we are a nation at war against terror.

This chapter reviews actions in what has come to be known as the "homeland security" domain that show that considerable instrumental policy learning did indeed take place after the September 11 attacks. This learning was not the result of some sort of newly initiated search for information and tools to address an emergent problem. Rather, in one day, members of the public and policymakers—the overwhelming majority of whom were not professional experts in homeland security issues—learned from experience that catastrophic terrorism was no longer simply a theoretical possibility. A wide range of assumptions had to be altered and policies changed to address the real threat of terrorist attack. These assumptions and policies were found wanting because nineteen terrorists had hijacked airplanes and turned them into guided missiles without their plot being effectively intercepted by the CIA, FBI, Defense Department, or any other law enforcement or national security agency.

To understand how the events of September 11 prompted learning, we must first explore the meaning of the term "homeland security," a term that first entered the public lexicon as a result of September 11. The concept of homeland security brings together a wide range of agencies and tools to address terrorist threats and that were virtually unknown to the public and to large parts of the government before the September 11 attacks. Until September 11, homeland security was the specialized domain of very few members of a particular policy elite.

We must also consider the history of domestic terrorism before September 11 and the policies intended to prevent or mitigate terrorism. A key part of this analysis is a summary of recommendations provided by two governmental commissions that provided a considerable amount of raw material on which policymakers could and did draw after September 11. And we must consider the September 11 attacks as focusing events by studying their impact on the policy agenda, and then look at the nature and substance of policy change after September 11. I contend that rapid policy change after September 11 was a function of both the magnitude of the attacks and the ready availability of potential policy options that could be rapidly implemented in their wake.

What Is Homeland Security?

Clearly, September 11 brought "homeland security" to the fore, but what exactly does this term mean? We can turn for guidance to the U.S. Commission on National Security/21st Century (also known as the Hart–Rudman Commission, after its cochairs). The Hart–Rudman Commission, which completed its phase I work before the September 11 attacks, found that "the U.S. will become increasingly vulnerable to hostile attacks in our homeland and that our military superiority will not entirely protect us" because such threats were not the type against which traditional intelligence gathering and defense could protect (U.S. Commission on National Security/21st Century 1999, 4). Furthermore, the commission found, in light of "rapid advances in information and biotechnology," new threats were emerging. The report argued that "there will be a blurring of boundaries: between homeland defense and foreign policy; between sovereign states and a plethora of protectorates and autonomous zones; and between the pull of national loyalties on individual citizens and the pull of loyalties both more local and more global in nature" (8).

In essence, we can say that homeland security is security against terrorist or other injurious attacks committed by nontraditional or nonstate actors, whose motives are different from conventional motives for making war. A key difficulty is that there is no one definition of terrorism and that any given definition is likely to be contested. It is often said, particularly in the context of colonized peoples throwing off their yoke, that one person's terrorist is another person's freedom fighter.[1] Still, for our purposes, the *Code of Federal Regulations* provides a useful definition of terrorism as including "the unlawful use of force or violence against persons or property to intimidate or coerce a Government, the civilian population, or any segment thereof, in furtherance of political or social objectives" (28 *CFR* 0.85[1]). This seems to be a workable definition; after all, it is important to understand how policymakers define the term, because their understanding is what is at issue here, and this definition, or some variant of it, is widely used in the federal government.

In recent years we have recognized that terrorism is emerging as a greater threat to national security than ever before, and certainly than we ever previously imagined. At the same time, collective security arrangements, the end of the cold war, and globalization and international economic interdependence have reduced the likelihood of interstate military conflict between superpowers or their alliance blocs (NATO and the Warsaw Pact, most prominently). Terrorist attacks are sometimes committed with the assistance or at least the tacit consent of state actors. The states that sponsor terrorism tend not to be great powers and have more to gain from what has come to be known as "asymmetric" conflicts. Such conflicts can be between large powerful states, on the one hand, and state-sponsored terrorist groups, state-tolerated terrorist groups, or groups with no state connection, on the other. Regardless of their sponsorship, terrorist groups generally are less interested in invading and controlling territory than they are in choosing targets of symbolic value, or for the disruptive effects an attack will have on a society. Terrorist attacks are intended to sow terror and confusion, and ultimately to undermine confidence in existing political leadership or even the existing legal and constitutional order.

Events and Reports: The Emergence of the Homeland Security Problem

Terrorist attacks are generally rare but when they happen they often kill many people, destroy property, and gain considerable mass and elite attention. Because they are so frightening and disruptive, major terrorist attacks have led to studies, commissions, and reports intended to analyze the most recent event and to recommend policy changes designed to prevent the recurrence of these attacks or to mitigate their effects once they happen. A timeline assembled by Claire B. Rubin, William B. Cumming, and Irmak R. Tanali displays key terrorist and other events, and the reports, response plans, legislation, executive directives, and other actions that followed those events and the subsequent policy-making activity.[2] This timeline shows that after most events reports are issued that describe the event and recommend policy responses. The window of opportunity for change and learning is therefore open. The September 11 attacks differ considerably from previous terrorist attacks in the United States, however, because studies and reports *followed* many of the policy responses to the attacks, rather than preceding and informing them. The September 11 attacks triggered reviews of analyses and recommendations made before the attacks. These pre–September 11 analyses were predicated on the assumption that a catastrophic, mass-casualty terrorist attack was likely to occur at some point somewhere in the United States. Of course, no one knew precisely when or where or exactly how such an attack would come. When the September 11 attacks occurred, the window of opportunity opened for actual policy change; indeed, the scale of the event demanded change. While the United States had experienced smaller-scale terrorism before, most recently with the bombing of the World Trade Center in 1993 and of the Murrah Federal Building in Oklahoma City in 1995, the September 11 attacks seemed to transform terrorism from a problem of law enforcement in the face of relatively small threats to a problem of national security on a potentially massive scale. Policymakers and citizens stopped merely thinking about the probability of a terrorist attack and began to express considerable concern about the possibility, however remote, of catastrophic terrorist attacks by groups using nuclear, chemical, or biological weapons.[3] Indeed, the October 2001 mailings of anthrax to news outlets and to members of Congress served to reinforce these fears of catastrophe.

The timeline of Rubin, Cumming, and Tanali begins in 1993, although a related narrative report begins its analysis in the 1980s (Rubin et al. 2003). The end of the cold war in 1991 is a crucial event, because it marked the beginning of a reassessment of U.S. military preparedness, capabilities, organization, and goals. In particular, the cold war notion of national security threats posed by states rather than nonstate or quasi state actors was not revised to take into account the threat posed by nonstate actors before September 11. The end of the cold war and the reordering based on economic strength rather than military might created a new security environment in which large-scale war became less likely and terrorism became a more prominent threat to national security. Many analysts were well aware of terrorist threats well before September 11, in large part because of their growing experience with terrorism, starting in the 1980s. The Iranian hostage crisis in 1979–81 and the bombing of the U.S. Marine barracks in Lebanon in October 1983 made clear even before the end of the cold war that terrorism against American interests—particularly terrorism perpetrated by individuals and groups claiming to act in the name of Islam—was becoming a growing threat. So-called Islamic terrorism was particularly vexing given American strategic interests in the Middle East and in south and central Asia. The appreciation of this threat grew in the 1990s with the bombing of the World Trade Center in 1993, the 1996 attack on the Khobar Towers housing complex in Dharan, Saudi Arabia (where American military personnel were housed), the attacks on the U.S. Embassies in Kenya and Tanzania in 1998, and the bombing of the U.S.S. *Cole* in 2000. The embassy and *Cole* attacks were blamed on al-Qaeda. The existence of this organization as a threat to the United States was therefore well known years before the September 11 attacks, which may explain why many policymakers and journalists assumed very quickly after the attacks—correctly, it appears—that al-Qaeda was the perpetrator of this crime.

Features of the cold war national security establishment included the location of military capabilities in the Department of Defense (DoD); diffuse intelligence and counterterrorism authorities and capabilities in the National Security Agency (NSA), CIA, DoD, and FBI; aviation security at the Federal Aviation Administration (FAA); and antiterrorist law enforcement in the Department of Justice (DOJ), of which the FBI is a part. Key national security functions were housed in the National Security Council (NSC), which by law included the president, vice president, and secretaries of state and defense. Statutory advisors to the NSC are the director of central intelligence (DCI) and the chairman of the Joint Chiefs of Staff (CJSC). Under Presidential Decision Directive 2, issued by President Bill Clinton on January 21, 1993, the NSC was enlarged to include the secretary of the treasury, the U.S. representative to the United Nations, the assistant to the president for national security affairs (typically known as the national security advisor), the assistant to the president for economic policy, and the president's chief of staff. On occasion, the attorney general would be a part of the NSC's meetings, and other officials were often invited as needed. A similar structure was retained under President Bush. When the Department of Homeland Security was created in 2003, the secretary of homeland security was not made a statutory member of the NSC, although this is not as large an omission as it may seem because not all presidents have made the NSC the centerpiece of their foreign policy or national security decision making.

This structure does reveal a great deal about the challenges confronting the national government in addressing potential threats to homeland security. A particular problem is the division between domestic and international intelligence. The abuses of the FBI and CIA, most notably during the Nixon administration but even before, under J. Edgar Hoover's leadership, led to the attorney general's adoption of guidelines designed to better regulate domestic intelligence gathering by the FBI. At the same time, the FBI disbanded its Domestic Intelligence Division. Subsequent attorneys general loosened the rules dividing the agencies, and in 1986 "Congress authorized the FBI to investigate terrorist attacks against Americans that occur outside the United States" (9/11 Commission 2004, 75). I consider more deeply below the understanding of terrorism as a problem for law enforcement rather than for the military. It is sufficient here to say that to the extent that terrorism was an issue in the United States in the 1980s, it was largely handled as a law enforcement matter.

As Lee Clarke has suggested and as Rubin and others have documented, the accumulation of reports, policies, and statutes is evidence that the threats brought to light by the September 11 attacks were already well known in advance. I focus on the two most important sets of reports, compiled in the late 1990s and early 2000s, which drew substantially on changes in policy and risk perception that developed in the 1990s. These reports were issued by the Gilmore and Hart–Rudman Commissions. Both of these efforts, begun before the September 11 attacks, were quite prescient about the issues that would confront policymakers after September 11. Indeed, decision makers drew upon these reports to shape policy after the September 11 attacks.

The Gilmore Commission

The Gilmore Commission's formal name was the "Advisory Panel to Assess Domestic Response Capabilities for Terrorism Involving Weapons of Mass Destruction." It was created under Section 1405 of the Strom Thurmond National Defense Authorization Act for Fiscal Year 1999, which called for it to be managed under contract with "a federally funded research and development center." This federally funded center was the RAND Corporation, a think tank with deep connections to the government. The commission's original charge was to meet from 1999 to 2001, but the September 11 attacks led to its being continued through five reports, the last of them issued in 2004. I am most interested in the ideas that were on the agenda before September 11.[4]

The Gilmore Commission focused primarily on the possibility of a mass-casualty attack using a CBRN (chemical, biological, radiological, or nuclear) device, and the government's ability to respond to such an attack. The term CBRN is preferred to the more common WMD (weapon of mass destruction) because the term WMD can be misleading in that it implies massive physical damage. A CBRN attack could kill thousands of people without doing massive structural damage. The Gilmore Commission's recommendations focused primarily on the detection and prevention of such attacks, including issues of response and cybersecurity. Cybersecurity was somewhat outside the commission's mandate, but the commission felt that other forms of security also depend on the security of the nation's information infrastructure.

The Hart–Rudman Commission

The Hart–Rudman Commission (formally known as the United States Commission on National Security/21st Century) published its report in three volumes, the majority of its recommendations in the final volume. Hart–Rudman took a broad view of homeland security, with a particular focus on the organization of the existing national security establishment in light of the threats outlined in the first two volumes of the report. Both the Gilmore and Hart–Rudman Commissions agreed that the threat of terrorism was increasing, that it was likely to come from fanatical religious groups, and that such groups, particularly in light of the 1995 sarin gas attacks in Tokyo, were likely to engage in mass-casualty terrorism, both to gain attention and to kill for the sake of killing.

In the third volume of its report, the Hart–Rudman Commission argued that the social and economic changes that accompany globalization, including the ease of international travel, greater transnational business links, and global interdependencies, mean that "the distinction between domestic and foreign no longer applies" (United States Commission on National Security/21st Century 2001, viii). Because international relations are no longer merely relations between nation-states (if they ever were), the emerging problem was one of homeland security—that is, safety within the nation's borders rather than national defense, which has traditionally focused on the maintenance of the nation's territorial sovereignty. The commission therefore called for the creation of a National Homeland Security Agency (NHSA) "with responsibility for planning, coordinating, and integrating various U.S. government activities involved in homeland security" (viii). The Federal Emergency Management Agency would form the core of such an agency, joined by the Coast Guard, the Customs Service, and the Border Patrol. The head of the NHSA would be a statutory advisor to the NSC, and "the legal foundation for the National Homeland Security Agency would rest firmly within the array of Constitutional guarantees for civil liberties. The observance of these guarantees in the event of a national security emergency would be safeguarded by NHSA's interagency *coordinating* activities, which would include the Department of Justice, as well as by its conduct of advance exercises" (viii, emphasis added). Among key additional recommendations was that Congress should create a single point of congressional oversight for homeland security rather than distribute oversight among multiple committees. Perhaps the most interesting thing about these recommendations is the explicit use of the term homeland security before the September 11 attacks. Indeed, the later adoption of this term is evidence of the influence that the commission had on policymaking after September 11.

It is useful to ask to what extent the Hart–Rudman and Gilmore Commissions anticipated the problems that were thrown into much sharper focus after the September 11 attacks. Table 2.1 lists the main categories of policies that these commissions addressed. Table 2.2 summarizes the topics of the recommendations made by these two commissions and by the 9/11 Commission. A bullet indicates that the commission made at least one recommendation in this area. In some cases, a commission made multiple recommendations for a particular category.

One may differ on the finer points of the definitions of each of these terms, but table 2.2 is not intended to be a statistical analysis. Rather, this table illustrates how the threat of terrorism was well known to people whose jobs required that they be concerned about the risks of terrorism before September 11. Before September 11 homeland security was a "policy without a public." Indeed, in the two years before September 11, "terrorism" was not even listed among the "most important problems" cited by respondents to Gallup polls on the issue. Clearly, the pre–September 11 record suggests that professionals in government, the military, academia,

Table 2.1 Policy Categories in the Homeland Security Domain

	9/11 Commission Categories[a]
War on Terror	Military attacks on terrorists, supporting states
Diplomacy	Efforts to build coalitions, deter states from sponsoring terrorism
Intelligence	Gathering and disseminating information about potential enemies and threats
Covert Action	Clandestine or covert actions to prevent attack, deter terrorists
Law Enforcement	Detection and prosecution of terrorism as a crime
Foreign Aid	Aid to nations to prevent conditions conducive to terrorism
Public Diplomacy	Public-image campaigns, broadcasting, and the like to develop positive image of the United States
Homeland Defense	Any effort undertaken within U.S. borders to detect, respond to, and recover from attacks
Oversight	Creation of committees or other structures in Congress to provide oversight over homeland security activities

Other Categories

Bioterrorism	Terrorism with biological agents
Border Security and Immigration	Proper issuance of visas, preventing illegal immigration
Cyber	Information security
Financing Terrorism	Tracking and cutting off terrorism funding
Human Resources	Training the people needed to combat terrorism
Identification	Positive identification systems
Organizational Change	Changes in the structure of existing organizations
Post–Cold War Changes to Military Structure	Changes to military posture in the post–cold war world
Private Preparedness	Private-sector activities to prepare for terrorist attacks
Risk Assessment	Systems to weigh risks to understand where terrorism is most likely to threaten the nation
Science, Technology, R&D	Research and development activities designed to detect, prevent, or mitigate attacks
State and Local Government	Response and recovery activities of first responders
Strategy	Development of a single national strategy to fight terrorism
Travel and Transportation	Means to prevent terrorists from traveling or attacking modes of transport

[a]"9/11 Commission Categories" are categories of policies explicitly mentioned in the commission's report. The "Other Categories" list includes issues not directly raised by the commission.

Table 2.2 Recommendations of the Hart–Rudman, Gilmore, and 9/11 Commissions

	Gilmore	Hart–Rudman	9/11
9/11 Commission Categories			
War on Terrorism	•	•	•
Diplomacy	•	•	•
Intelligence	•	•	•
Covert Action			•
Law Enforcement			•
Foreign Aid		•	•
Public Diplomacy			•
Homeland Defense	•	•	•
Oversight	•	•	•
Other Categories			
Bioterrorism	•		
Border Security and Immigration			•
Cyber	•		
Financing Terrorism			•
Human Resources		•	•
Identification			•
Organizational Change	•	•	•
Post–Cold War Changes to Military Structure		•	
Private Preparedness			•
Risk Assessment		•	
Science, Technology, R&D	•	•	
State and Local Government	•	•	
Strategy	•		
Travel and Transportation		•	

and think tanks paid attention to domestic terrorism, but the public gave it little if any attention. There was little incentive, therefore, for Congress to become too exercised over the issue. Before September 11 Congress paid much more attention to flight delays and poor airline service than to potential terrorist attacks on aviation.

The September 11 Attacks as Focusing Events

Among those whose job it was to care about terrorism, the emergent threat of terrorism within the borders of the United States was clearly very salient. What was missing from this policy domain was a sense of urgency about the possibility of catastrophic terrorism because it was not clear whether or when an international terrorist group could mount an attack on the scale of the September 11 attacks. September 11 provided that sense of urgency because it was a focusing event. It was a rare event, it caught both the public and many (but not all) elite policymakers by surprise (which is more important than the difference between elite and mass perceptions of the *probability* of the threat), it killed thousands of people and did billions of dollars' worth of damage, and it revealed vulnerabilities across a wide spectrum of policy areas related in more or less direct ways to what we now call homeland security.

Further evidence of the role of the September 11 attacks as focusing events comes from contemporary claims that the event was a pivotal moment in U.S. history. The importance of the September 11 attacks as a rationale and trigger for policy change was expressed in several news articles (Fenlon and Lee-Shanock 2001; Stephenson 2001; Woodlief 2001). These articles reinforced the theme expressed in the lead sentence of an article in an Ottawa, Ontario, newspaper: "The terrorist attack on the United States is the sort of historic event that permanently changes the way people think" (Robson 2001). Furthermore, an ABC News/*Washington Post* poll conducted in March 2002, six months after the attacks, found that "the vast majority of Americans, 86 percent, say the events of September 11 have changed the nation in a lasting way" (Langer 2002).

In Congress the theme of change was also voiced, often in ways that would justify changes in attitudes or policies. For example, Representative Scott McInnis (R-CO) argued in the *Congressional Record,* "the world changed on September 11. The days of being absolutely politically correct, the days of Harvard not allowing the U.S. military, the ROTC on their campus, those days are gone" (McInnis 2001, H 6899). However, Senator Patrick Leahy (D-VT) noted in the *Congressional Record* that "It has been said over and over that 'the world has changed.' . . . Our response to this tragedy is causing changes throughout our society. However, in another sense, it has a lot more to do with our perceptions of the world than with the world itself. The world was changing long before September 11, and threats that existed before that infamous day are no less present today" (Leahy 2001, S. 11357).

Two positions were staked out in Congress and reflected in policymaking: one that implied that the September 11 attacks changed the actual nature and probability of an attack by international terrorists, and another that suggested that the attacks merely changed our perceptions of the risk in a way that made substantial policy change possible. I take the second position. While the events of September 11 provided the impetus for change, the threat of terrorism was already well established in the policy stream, and September 11 only threw open the window of opportunity for policy change based in large part on preexisting ideas. Senator Leahy's argument is consistent with Kingdon's contention that problems and policies exist somewhat independently of each other but can coalesce when a window of opportunity opens. Indeed, Congress's increased attention to terrorism was much less pronounced than the media's sudden interest because Congress had already been at least somewhat attentive to the issue. The news media, by contrast, were generally inattentive to the terrorist threat. Indeed, the news media had been so focused on "soft" news before September 11 that the attacks triggered a wave of news coverage that served both as a monument to what journalists and journalism can do and as a way of shaming the news industry for its lack of seriousness before the event. Some have even argued that the line between news and entertainment had become so blurred that the two were indistinguishable (Rosen 2002).

While it may be obvious that the September 11 attacks were major agenda-setting events, it is important to understand just how large an influence these events had on the agenda. I will consider both media and congressional agendas to look at how these attacks expanded what we might call the "terrorism" agenda in both these institutions. I start by considering the nature of agenda expansion in the mass media, using the *New York Times* as a measure.

Figure 2.1 shows index scores of stories on the term "terrorism" in the *New York Times* by year, from 1990 to mid-2002. I found these stories by searching the term "terrorism" in the keywords or lead paragraphs of these stories. The stories are listed by the "desk" from which they originated, which helps us determine whether the *Times* treated the story as a metropolitan, national, or world issue. The figure also shows the number of people who testified about terrorism before Congress as a measure of Congress's attention to the issue. The index has been normalized, so the mean number of stories per desk per year or witnesses per year from 1990 to 2000 equals 100. This allows for comparisons across desks that would be harder to see with the raw numbers alone.[5]

Whereas there were at least three terrorist or terror-like incidents between 1990 and 2001—the first bombing of the World Trade Center, the 1995 Oklahoma City bombing, and the Olympic Park bombing in Atlanta during the 1996 Olympics—the September 11 attacks created a volume of stories far greater than any of these other events. Clearly, the September 11 attacks "brought home" the issue of international terrorism as a problem of national security rather than primarily an international problem. The event also increased sensitivity to terrorism in foreign news reporting, although clearly not as dramatically. Unique features of the 1993 World Trade Center and 1995 Oklahoma City bombings are also evident. The 1993 attack had a much greater influence on the local news agenda than it did on the national agenda, while the 1995 Oklahoma City bombing elevated terrorism to the highest level it had ever reached on the national news agenda before September 11.

Figure 2.1 shows the dramatic effect of the event on the national news agenda. It also shows that news coverage of the September 11 events follows, in at least some respects, the "issue-attention cycle," in which the news media cover an issue aggressively but briefly, coverage abating as the event recedes and as political institutions act or fail to act in substantive or symbolic ways (Downs 1972). However, one cannot say that news coverage of terrorism has returned to pre–September 11 levels. National coverage of the issue did rise again in 2004, in large part because of the presidential election campaign. In 2005 we saw more coverage of terrorism across all the *Times*'s various desks than we've seen since 2001.

Figure 2.1   Stories on "Terrorism" in the *New York Times*, by Desk, 1990–2004, with Congressional Testimony on Terrorism

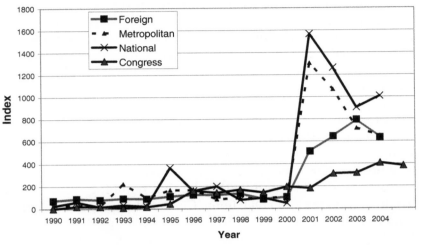

Source: LexisNexis search for the term "terrorism" in headline, lead, or key terms, by desk; testimony in LexisNexis congressional testimony database, by term "terrorism."

Like the news media, Congress has paid a great deal of attention to the September 11 attacks, but the expansion of the congressional agenda was not as great as the increase in media attention. This difference reveals well-established institutional differences between the news media and Congress. A finer-scale analysis of the data shows that a significant increase in news coverage of terrorism occurred in the two weeks after September 11, followed by a substantial drop-off in coverage after that first fortnight. News coverage of terrorism as a national issue remains high, but it has never returned to the levels reached in those first two weeks. Congress, on the other hand, saw its terrorism agenda expand continuously in the six weeks following September 11, and this expansion continued through 2004. This reflects the difference between Congress as a decision-making and deliberative body that had already begun to show some concern about terrorism, and the media, which treated domestic terrorism as an extraordinary event to which saturation coverage was devoted for a relatively short time.

We can say with confidence that the September 11 attacks were, collectively, a focusing event that had a profound impact on the media and congressional agendas. Widespread attention was paid to the threat of terrorism after the September 11 attacks, and attention remains quite high. Nevertheless, attention, as policy scholars know, is different from policy change.

September 11, Policy Failure, Learning, and Change

The question is whether policy change after September 11 reflects evidence of learning, or whether policy change was simply the result of superstitious learning, mimicking, or merely the desire to "do something" under the pressure of events, without proper analysis and design.

As I argued in *After Disaster,* focusing events lead to widespread claims of policy failure: The event itself is evidence that policy failed to prevent a tragedy from occurring. The rhetoric of policy failure was prominent in Congress after September 11. Senator Jay Rockefeller (D-WV) noted in his discussion of a proposed Aviation Security Act, "The truth is, the horrific attacks of September 11 do reflect broad intelligence and other failures."[6] Other comments on this failure include the following:

- "Simply put, the private contractors who currently have the responsibility for screening passengers and baggage failed on September 11, and for that matter, they have failed for the past three decades" (Millender-McDonald 2001).
- "Mr. Speaker, evidence continues to mount that we suffered a major, major failure of intelligence prior to September 11" (Miller 2002).
- "Mr. Chairman, the great failure of September 11 was our failure to methodically analyze and share among our Federal and local authorities critical intelligence information" (Bishop 2002).

There were several subjective and objective manifestations of policy failure after the attacks: apparent failures of intelligence and information sharing, failures in aviation security screening, even the structural failure of the World Trade Center towers as a result of what was claimed to be insufficient or improperly applied fireproofing on the steel members of the building. But perhaps more important than the individual policy failures is the more fundamental change in the social construction of the terrorist problem itself. Changes in the appreciation of how problems come about, what causes them, and what can be done to change the conditions under which they grow worse are central to understanding social policy learning.

Shifting Constructions of the Terrorist Threat

An important part of this social policy learning process was the post–September 11 rejection of law enforcement as the primary tool for attacking terrorists. Before September 11 terrorism was considered more a crime than an act of war. Most of the bombers and their direct coconspirators in the World Trade Center bombing in 1993 were apprehended and punished through a combination of excellent detective work by the FBI and the ineptitude of the bombers, who left clues to their identity. As the 9/11 Commission noted, "An unfortunate consequence of this superb investigative and prosecutorial effort was that it created an impression that the law enforcement system was well equipped to cope with terrorism. . . . [T]he successful use of the legal system to address the first World Trade Center bombing had the side effect of obscuring the need to examine the character and extent of the new threat facing the United States" (9/11 Commission 2004, 72).

After September 11, the preferred approach to fighting terrorism shifted from law enforcement to "homeland security," with its echoes of "national security," a function closely identified with the use of military and to some extent diplomatic power, rather than with criminal trials. As the 9/11 Commission noted, law enforcement solutions presume that one can detect a crime, find the perpetrators, and punish them, thereby ending the matter. Counterterrorism, the commission argued, requires that efforts be made to detect plots before they occur, to discern patterns that might uncover additional plots, and to predict the time, place, and manner of future attacks. The attacks also seemed to indicate that a static defense strategy based on law enforcement would not deter or prevent terrorist attacks, and that a much more aggressive posture was necessary.

Post–September 11 Legislation as Evidence of Instrumental Learning

It is hardly surprising that a great deal of legislation was introduced after September 11. The attacks led to a broad range of legislation, summarized in table 2.3. The number of bills is quite remarkable; no fewer than thirty-two new laws have been enacted since the September 11 attacks, among them the Homeland Security Act, the Transportation Security and Aviation Stabilization Act, and the controversial USA PATRIOT Act. Rather than merely list the bills, table 2.3 assigns them to the categories suggested by the 9/11 Commission's report, which noted that there is more to homeland security than the "war on terrorism." "The first phase of our post-9/11 efforts rightly included military action to topple the Taliban and pursue al Qaeda. This work continues. But long-term success demands the use of all elements of national power: diplomacy, intelligence, covert action, law enforcement, economic policy, foreign aid, public diplomacy, and homeland defense. If we favor one tool while neglecting others, we leave ourselves vulnerable and weaken our national effort" (9/11 Commission 2004, 363–64).

The greatest volume of legislation that passed into law fell primarily under the "homeland defense" category. Within the broad categories outlined by the 9/11 Commission, there has been substantive change in law enforcement powers, bioterrorism, cybersecurity, and aviation security. These issues had been raised in both the Hart–Rudman and Gilmore reports, but no legislation had been enacted. The events of September 11 enabled rapid legislative changes that addressed these areas. The September 11 attacks transformed terrorism from an abstract concern to a very real problem. It also changed the behavior of political actors by allowing them, and all American citizens, to comprehend the seriousness of terrorist threats.

As remarkable as the relatively rapid pace of policy change was after September 11, there is little evidence that the attacks triggered any real policy innovation. That is, most of the policy ideas had already been articulated by the intelligence and policy

Table 2.3 Public Laws Related to Terrorism, September 2001–December 2004

Category	Definition	No. of Laws	Examples
War on Terrorism	Military action against terrorists and terrorist organizations	5	Authorize use of force against those responsible for the recent attacks, PL 107-40 Became PL 107-56 Became PL 107-287
Intelligence	Improved systems for collecting, analyzing, and sharing information about terrorist threats and groups	2	Intelligence Reform and Terrorism Prevention Act of 2004, PL 108-458
Law Enforcement	Changes to the law, procedures, and the like, to detect and prosecute terrorism and related acts as crimes	3	USA PATRIOT Act, PL 107-56
Diplomacy and Foreign Aid	Efforts to support friendly governments and to promote U.S. interests in nations around the world	3	Authorize the president to exercise waivers of foreign assistance restrictions with respect to Pakistan through September 30, 2003, and for other purposes, PL 107-57
Homeland Defense	Measures to prevent, prepare for, and mitigate potential terrorist attacks	13	Homeland Security Act of 2003, PL 107-296; Aviation and Transportation Security Act, PL 107-71; Cyber Security Research and Development Act, PL 107-305; Public Health Security and Bioterrorism Preparedness and Response Act of 2002, PL 107-188

Source: Congress's Thomas search engine bill file, http://thomas.loc.gov (search for term *terrorism*). Some bills can span more than one category owing to their breadth, such as the Homeland Security Act. Bills that are largely symbolic (such as memorials) are excluded.

experts. The creation of a homeland security agency and the more systematic collection of intelligence information were key recommendations of the Hart–Rudman Commission. Moreover, the Patriot Act encompassed much of the conservative law enforcement community's preexisting desires for more aggressive law enforcement tools, such as new rules for wiretapping in the face of the profusion of new communications methods and for seizing the property of suspected criminals, goals that arguably had little to do with the new "war on terror." "The sense that the administration is using the war on terrorism to accomplish long-held policy goals is not limited to liberals. 'They are taking language off the shelf that's been ready to go into any vehicle,' said Roger Pilon, vice president for legal affairs at the Cato Institute, the libertarian research group. He was particularly critical of a provision the administration inserted into the USA PATRIOT Act that enhanced the government's ability to seize assets through forfeiture" (Greenhouse 2002).

This is consistent with Kingdon's argument that existing ideas are combined with new problems or new appreciations of problems when windows of opportunity are open. And this is also consistent with May's (1992) conception of "political learning," in which political actors learn which social constructions and rhetorical tools are most likely to win acceptance of a policy position; these arguments usually have little to do with the policy instruments or the objective causes of problems.

The failure to innovate after September 11 is not by itself evidence of a failure to learn. After all, Busenberg's definition of learning, as we saw, is "a process in which individuals apply new information and ideas to policy decisions." Peter May's definition of instrumental policy learning does not require innovation; it only requires that policymakers learn "lessons about the viability of policy instruments or implementation designs" (1992, 331). New information and new ways of appreciating the viability of policy instruments came in two forms. The first was the appreciation of al-Qaeda as a much greater threat to the United States at home than had been previously acknowledged, particularly by the Bush administration. Whereas al-Qaeda was clearly near the top of analysts' concerns about international terrorism, it was not yet clear that al-Qaeda could or would mount the sort of attack that it did on September 11.

The second form of information was a broader change in the perception of risk from terrorism after the most ruthless and destructive terrorist attack in U.S. history. From a policy change perspective, the issue of terrorism became more salient, even though the actual nature of the threat and the probability of its occurrence did not change suddenly on September 11. Policy shifted from measures intended to address a potential future threat that could potentially be thwarted to policy that was intended to react to a clear and obvious threat. The graphically obvious nature of this threat—exemplified most clearly by the destruction of the World Trade Center—was so compelling that this new information triggered the generation of new ideas about what was possible in terrorism. Rather than being concerned with the usual truck bombings, broad segments of the American public safety and security apparatus became concerned about the prospects of catastrophic nuclear, biological, or chemical terrorism. After all, the reasoning went, if terrorists were willing to do something as ghastly as the September 11 attacks, were there any restraints on their behavior? It appeared that there were no restraints. Indeed, this change in risk perception was caused by an event so profound that catastrophic terrorism was, for most members of Congress and the public, a largely new idea, not just new information about an old idea. Regardless of what September 11 represented, it is fair to say that post–September 11 policy changes constituted instrumental learning.

The Role of the 9/11 Commission in Instrumental Learning

My claim that there is evidence of instrumental learning is further bolstered by the findings of the 9/11 Commission, which issued its final report in 2004. This report revealed major gaps in the nation's immigration, intelligence, aviation security, and other systems. The commission claimed that without rapid administration and congressional response to its recommendations, the nation would be at considerable risk. It also noted that action had already begun on ideas that predated the September 11 attacks, such as the creation of a single homeland security agency and improved aviation security measures.

The relatively poor record of implementing the recommendations of presidential commissions on aviation security (discussed in chapter 3) and the history of many other issues that were studied and then ignored by special commissions may well have fueled speculation that the 9/11 Commission's recommendations themselves would be ignored. "'My worst nightmare is this report will be collecting dust on a shelf somewhere,' said Robin Wiener, a Washington lobbyist who lost her brother, Jeff, in the World Trade Center collapse" (Alberts 2004).

The national mood, to use Kingdon's term, after September 11 demanded some sort of honest response to the commission's recommendations in light of relatively high public interest in the commission, interest that may have been spurred by the politics of its creation. For example, in a CBS News poll on April 9, 2004, 61 percent of those responding indicated that they were "very closely" or "somewhat closely" attentive to the commission's hearings.[7] The belief that the president was cooperating with the commission broke along party lines, with 79 percent of Republicans but only 42 percent of Democrats indicating a belief that "the White House is . . . cooperating with the hearings investigating the September 11 terrorist attacks on the United States." The 9/11 Commission and its recommendations were very much in play in a politically charged election year. The Bush administration would have run serious political risks if it sought to ignore the commission altogether, given the widespread belief—based on solid evidence—that the Bush administration did not want the 9/11 Commission to be created.

The commission was created in spite of Bush's opposition, and it held a series of public hearings that were well covered by the national news media, particularly when controversial subjects like the Bush administration's response to the terrorist threat were on the agenda. Given this widespread attention to terrorism generally and to the commission in particular, the commission's recommendations had to be taken seriously by the administration and Congress. In this case, political pressure forced Congress and the president to act more quickly than they initially seemed inclined to do.

It initially appeared that Congress would fail to take up the recommendations of the report until after it returned from its August recess. But the political pressure—whether a product of elite action, media exposure, or public outcry—resulted in Congress holding August hearings to address the recommendations of the report. Another unusual tactic of this commission was that its members fanned out across the nation to press for the adoption of its key recommendations. By contrast, the chairs of the commissions that dealt with aviation security after the two key aviation security incidents of the 1990s appeared once each before Congress, in a relatively perfunctory way, and were never as publicly visible in as wide a range of venues as were the members of the 9/11 Commission.

Commission chairman Thomas Kean, former governor of New Jersey, famously noted that the failure to thwart the September 11 attacks was the result of a "failure of imagination," given the number of similar earlier plots to use hijacked airplanes to commit acts of catastrophic terrorism. The 9/11 Commission did not uncover this failure, nor did it initially elevate it as an issue on the policy agenda. The attacks themselves had far greater agenda-setting power, although one might attribute the increase in attention to terrorism in 2004 to ongoing media coverage of the commission's hearings. However, the 9/11 Commission had a considerable amount of moral authority that, when combined with interest groups such as Families of September 11, representing victims' families, was available to force policymakers into action. In addition, Kean's commitment to pursue the recommendations of the commission was a departure from the usual model of Washington commissions. The 9/11 Commission departed from the norm in that it was created during a period of considerable controversy. In the face of opposition from the executive branch and some members of the legislative branch, it continued its work and vowed to bring public pressure to bear on implementing its recommendations, rather than simply issuing its report and folding its tent.

Much of what the commission recommended has been implemented in some form. The major legislative accomplishment that followed the September 11 attacks was the enactment of the Intelligence Reform and Terrorism Prevention Act of 2004 (PL 108-458) on December 17, 2004. The key provision of this act was the creation of a new position, the director of national intelligence (DNI), who would be responsible for the collection of intelligence from all sources, including the CIA and the military. Curiously, this role was originally carved out for the director of central intelligence (DCI) and the CIA, but it had become clear well before September 11 that the CIA was anything but "central" to the collection of intelligence. Indeed, the failure of intelligence sharing contributed to the failure of the United States to detect the September 11 plot. The goal of the 2004 act, therefore, was to force this information sharing through the offices of the DNI. The DNI replaced the DCI as the president's key briefer on intelligence matters, and the DCI (whose title is now the director of the Central Intelligence Agency, or DCIA) and CIA are now subordinate to the DNI. This structure is similar to the structure called for by the 9/11 Commission, which sought to create a deputy DNI who would run the CIA and be more closely tied bureaucratically to the DNI.

The Office of the DNI (ODNI) is a stand-alone agency with quasi cabinet status. The DNI is not a statutory member of the NSC. These features of the DNI's position (filled by Ambassador John Negroponte in early 2005) have created doubt about the actual power that the DNI will have; it appears clear that the level of his power will be determined by the president, who must continue to direct the other intelligence agencies to report to the DNI. This organizational change was the key element of instrumental policy change that followed the 9/11 Commission's report. Time will tell whether the recommendations will be effectively implemented and whether this new structure—as well as the others put in place between September 11 and the issuance of the commission's report—will be effective in thwarting threats to the homeland.

Conclusions: Learning after September 11

The September 11 attacks were the historical turning point in policy change relating to homeland security and triggered a period of instrumental and social policy change. They illustrated the very real phenomenon of mass-casualty terrorism in the United States and fired the imaginations of policymakers across the board, who began to ask whether there could be worse terrorist attacks on the horizon. The September 11 attacks were followed, in October 2001, by a set of mailings of anthrax spores to government officials and members of the news media. The combined effect of September 11 and the anthrax mailings led people to think far outside the normal realm of possibility and to consider the possibility of biological, chemical, or radiological terrorism, ranging from chemicals or pathogens to dirty bombs and perhaps even the detonation of a nuclear weapon. September 11 seems to have made the "unthinkable" thinkable to a broad range of people in government, the media, and the public domain generally. While most of these threats were well known and some measures had been taken to address them, September 11 made the issue of terrorism much more salient to a broad range of people.

This broad sense of what was possible in terrorism facilitated instrumental and social policy learning. If successfully applied, social policy learning can result in better understanding of the underlying causal theory of a public problem, and can lead to improved policy responses. Prima facie indicators of social policy learning include "policy redefinition entailing changes in policy goals or scope—e.g., policy direction, target groups, rights bestowed by the policy" (May 1992). It is reasonable to conclude that the result of the September 11 attacks was a thorough review of what terrorism means and how the United States should respond to it.

The learning process after the September 11 attacks was unusual. The attacks triggered a remarkable period of policymaking without the usual study commissions or other deliberative mechanisms that are often employed after focusing events. Action after the September 11 attacks was rapid because of their manifest seriousness. Members of Congress and the executive branch hardly needed a report to tell them that September 11 was a serious event. The public pressure to "do something" after the event also drove policymaking. Much of what was done was largely symbolic. Symbolic actions included resolutions condemning the attack and recognizing the heroism of first responders and others. These symbolic expressions generally give way very quickly—in this case, by the end of the 107th Congress—as Congress shifted to considering substantive policy change.

This is not to say, however, that substantive policy action has been fully thought out. The creation of the DHS, in terms of budget and personnel, is perhaps the largest manifestation of the pressure to do something, regardless of how well thought out. The wisdom of creating such a large and unwieldy agency has been questioned in both the popular and academic press. While some of this criticism is a function of the critics' perception of who was winning or losing in the creation of the department, much of it is the inevitable result of pursuing such a daunting task as coordinating so many groups into an agency with a shared mission. This will be particularly challenging given that that terrorist attacks are rare events, while the daily tasks of processing airline passengers and immigrants, monitoring plant and animal diseases, and patrolling coastal waters involve functions that do not directly support an antiterrorism or homeland security mission as defined by the DHS.

In terms of the model presented in chapter 1, it is clear that the September 11 attacks generated considerable attention. What is not clear is the extent to which group mobilization led to what I call in the model the "discernible discussion of ideas." It appears that there was relatively little interest group mobilization that led to policy change, in large part because some sort of policy change was a foregone conclusion after September 11; the pace of change between September 11 and the end of 2001 was remarkable. The attacks were so spectacular that they made their own case for some sort of policy change; they did not require a lot of group mobilization to help Congress understand or interpret them. This claim is at best provisional, however, because I have not delved deeply into the congressional hearings in the homeland security domain to understand the nature and extent of group mobilization. As we will see in chapter 3, however, the dominant group representatives that appeared before congressional hearings on aviation security matters were representatives of the federal government. There is little reason to suspect that the homeland security domain more broadly would be much different; the sorts of decisions made in this domain tend to be those for which federal officials are responsible. Moreover, it is clear from the wide range of issues that were addressed in potential legislation and in the three commission reports reviewed here that terrorist attacks do mobilize ideas in the policy process.

To conclude, there is evidence of instrumental and social policy learning after the September 11 attacks. The existence of many "off the shelf" ideas in circulation before September 11 made the adoption of new policy instruments much easier. The adoption of new policy tools based on learning awaited a focusing event to open the window of opportunity for policy change. These findings further buttress existing public policy theory that suggests that few new ideas emerge, even in the wake of focusing events, but that new facts combine with old ideas in windows of opportunity for change. In the two case studies that follow, I consider further the question of whether instrumental learning is based on new ideas or on the repackaging and reconfiguring of existing ideas and preferred policy options.

three

learning from aviation security disasters

I examine aviation security, a particular aspect of homeland security, for several reasons. First, the issue existed long before the term "homeland security" entered the lexicon. In the United States, aviation security measures such as passenger screening date to the rash of hijackings in the 1970s. Before the widespread use of metal detectors, criminals and terrorists found aviation an attractive target for attacks. Second, the contours of the policy domain are fairly well defined, with the roles of the various actors—the government, airlines, the traveling public—well known to all participants. This clear definition of the problems and who is involved in addressing them makes it easy to study event-related change and learning. Third, I focus on aviation security because the failure to prevent terrorists from hijacking planes and crashing them into buildings can be thought of as the ultimate policy failure in a chain of intelligence failures and failures to enforce immigration laws. It is reasonable to argue that, had the aviation security system provided the security that its defenders—the airlines and the Federal Aviation Administration—claimed it did, the World Trade Center would still be standing today. But the system failed to keep terrorists off the planes, out of the cockpits, and away from the controls. The results were so significant that one can reasonably expect that some sort of response would follow this security failure.

The hijacking of four airplanes in one day, in a nation that had long believed in the superior security of its commercial aviation sector, would have been a historic and deeply alarming event even if the hijackings had fit the classic pattern. In the typical hijacking, an airplane is seized, passengers and crew are taken hostage, and the airplane is forced to land at one or more places for fuel, supplies, and perhaps to free some passengers. In most cases negotiations succeed in releasing all or most of the hostages, even if the plane is eventually destroyed. Sometimes, as in the famous 1976 Israeli action at Entebbe, Uganda, the plane is stormed by police or military forces. This pattern was shattered on September 11, 2001. The hijackers, having planned and trained for years, seized planes with the intention of using them as guided missiles against symbolically important targets. I will argue that the threat of such an attack was not as novel as some commentators have suggested. Nevertheless, the shock of the event and its apparent novelty at the time combine to make this one of the most pivotal events in modern American history.

While chapter 2 showed that the September 11 attacks influenced a broad range of policies, in this chapter I assume that the September 11 attacks were fundamentally about the nearly simultaneous hijacking of four U.S. flag airliners in domestic airspace and their use as guided missiles that collectively killed more than twenty-eight hundred people. Had the nineteen hijackers been prevented from taking flight training, secreting weapons on their person or on the planes, boarding the airplanes, attacking the crew and passengers, or gaining access to the flight deck, the September 11 attacks would not have been as grave. There have been enough other bombings and hijackings of planes—American and otherwise—in the past forty years that attacks against civil aviation, even one similar to the September 11 attack, could hardly be called unexpected. We should therefore consider whether anything was learned before September 11 that should have reduced the likelihood of these attacks and, perhaps more important, whether September 11 contained any lessons that have been successfully applied to improve aviation security. While it may well be true that not all attacks can be prevented, one can also argue that any system that allows four hijackings in one day has significant flaws. If nothing else, the September 11 hijackings provided the aviation security community with an unparalleled learning opportunity.

It has long been known that aviation security is critical to the operation of a reliable, trustworthy system of air transportation, both within a nation and in international trade and commerce. The aviation sector accounts for about 9 percent of the United States' gross domestic product (Thomas 2003), and a sufficient number of security breaches would probably dissuade many people from flying, as happened in the immediate wake of the September 11 attacks. A key indicator of air traffic—revenue seat miles flown—declined sharply in 2001 and did not rebound to pre-2001 levels until 2004. The September 11 attacks accelerated problems in the industry already beset by expensive labor agreements, high fuel costs, stiff price competition, and in some cases an excess number of seats.

Fortunately, fatal aviation security breaches are still relatively rare compared with the huge number of passengers and tons of freight carried daily, but successful attacks on civil aviation are sufficiently spectacular when they do happen to generate considerable mass and elite concern. The September 11 attacks are the only terrorist or seemingly terrorist-related incidents that have had an independent effect on the key indicators of airline performance over a long period. The attacks reinforced the idea that civil aviation is a desirable target for terrorists, and they revealed why it is in everyone's interest—passengers, airlines, the travel industry in general, and regulators—to ensure that the aviation security system prevents fatal attacks.

Historical Trends in Aviation Security

The intentional destruction of aircraft in flight is not unheard of in the United States. According to the database maintained at www.airdisaster.com, at least four U.S. civil airliners have been bombed in American airspace, and at least one crashed owing to the actions of a disgruntled former pilot. At the same time, air travel has grown to the point that by 2005, according to a *Newsweek* poll, 77 percent of Americans had flown on a commercial airliner at least once. This mode of transportation passed from something only "jet-setters" used to a near-universal form of intercity and international transportation in about forty years. The prospect of terrorist attacks on commercial aviation is horrifying in its own right and has become a crime that strikes more fear into a broader range of Americans than it would have in the early years of commercial aviation.

The number of airliner bombings, hijackings, suicide attacks, and other crimes against commercial aviation is striking (Merari 1999) both in terms of the long history of these attacks and the relative newness of policy responses. The first attempted hijacking occurred in 1931, but the most public manifestation of the hijacking problem came with the rash of hijackings of planes to Cuba in the 1960s and early 1970s. One sensational hijacking took place in 1972; "D. B. Cooper" hijacked a domestic flight, collected ransom for the plane, and jumped out the back stairs of a 727 flying over rugged land between Seattle and Portland, never to be seen again (although his money washed up years later). Hijackings in other nations have also occurred for economic or political reasons, but we are now in an era where most attacks against commercial aviation worldwide are done for political reasons by terrorists (St. John 1999). As a result of the hijackings in the late 1960s and early 1970s, authorities became most concerned about weapons being used to hijack planes, so the first metal detectors were installed in airports. Hijackings in United States airspace subsequently became quite rare, and states like Cuba began to deal sternly with hijackers.

The next wave of terrorist attacks on aircraft came in the mid-1980s, when high-profile bombings directed worldwide attention to the aviation security problem. Since the advent of this more violent era of aircraft bombings, three events have dominated aviation security policy in the United States. These events were the Pan Am Flight 103 bombing over Lockerbie, Scotland, in 1988, the loss of TWA Flight 800 off Long Island, New York, in 1996 (which was not, as it turned out, the result of terrorist action), and the September 11 hijackings. The details of these events are well known and have been covered in other contexts, so I will not go into detail here.[1] I summarize these events in table 3.1, which provides background on four key elements of each event: the facts of the event itself, a description of the ultimate cause as generally agreed upon by elite decision makers and mainstream journalists, a summary of alternate theories of the causes of these events, and a summary of the policy responses to these events. Ideas for dealing with threats to aviation security have been on various agendas in the United States since at least the Pan Am 103 disaster, but policy change was generally incremental until the September 11 attacks cast a harsh light on the now well-known failures of the aviation security system.

In the wake of these three events, members of Congress, investigating commissions, government agencies, and interest groups debated what seems to be a straightforward issue: how to keep attackers and bombs off airplanes. The popular, trade, and academic literature broadly agrees that aviation security was successful in a statistical sense in the United States even in light of the September 11 attacks.[2] After all, the vast majority of civil airliners are not bombed or hijacked every day. However, this probabilistic approach to aviation security fails to engage the possibilistic thinking described by Lee Clarke (Clarke 2005a, 2005b). Possibilistic thinking considers not the statistical probability of an unlikely event but the very bad consequences that *could* result if such an unlikely event happens—and unlikely events, Clarke notes, happen far more often than we might want to believe.

The conclusion one ordinarily reaches after reviewing the history of this domain is that policymakers in aviation security failed to consider adequately the possibility of a catastrophic failure of the system, even as evidence accumulated that enemies of the United States were planning an attack and that the aviation security system was flawed. The September 11 attacks fit the definition of a "high-consequence/low-probability event" that may seem unimaginable or difficult to prevent but that deserves considerable effort to prevent because of the magnitude of its consequences. Indeed, as I argued in chapter 2, the September 11 attacks changed our perception of both the probability of catastrophic terrorist attacks on the United States—or elsewhere, for that matter—and our perception of the likely consequences of such attacks. Mass-casualty terrorism in the United States thereby passed from the realm of speculation to reality.

Table 3.1 Key Features of Aviation Security Incidents

Event	What Happened	Dominant Causal Story	Alternate Causal Stories	Policy Responses
Pan Am 103, December 21, 1988	Pan Am Boeing 747 bound for New York explodes over Lockerbie, Scotland, killing all aboard and 11 on the ground.	Bomb planted by two members of the Libyan secret services, perhaps in retaliation against Anglo-American strikes on Libya in 1986.	Syrian terrorists	August 14, 1989: President George H. W. Bush issued Executive Order 12686, which formed the Presidential Commission on Aviation Security and Terrorism. May 1990: Commission presents findings, stating that there were serious flaws in the aviation security system. November 16, 1990: Aviation Security Improvement Act (PL 101-604, 104 Stat. 3066)

TWA 800, July 16, 1996	TWA Boeing 747 explodes minutes after leaving JFK Airport bound for Paris.	Empty center fuel tank, full of fumes and overheated from sitting on the ground on a hot day and from nearby air conditioning unit, explodes when a spark is introduced into the tank, possibly from fuel level equipment.	Terrorist bomb; terrorist missile; errant U.S. Navy missile	Federal Aviation Reauthorization Act of 1996 (PL 104-264)
September 11, 2001, terrorist attacks	Four cross-country flights—two out of Newark, NJ, and two out of Boston—are hijacked. One crashes into the Pentagon, two into the World Trade Center, utterly destroying that facility, and one crashes in Pennsylvania as a result of a passenger uprising against the hijackers.	Hijackers introduced weapons onto planes, somehow passing through security. The hijackers were part of the al-Qaeda terrorist organization led by Osama bin Laden.	No alternative theories were offered that were taken seriously: some conspiracy theories about Israel, etc.	Air Transportation Safety and System Stabilization Act (PL 107-42); Aviation and Transportation Security Act (PL 107-71); Homeland Security Act of 2002 (PL 107-296)

Since the spate of hijackings in the 1980s, and particularly beginning with the post–Pan Am 103 and TWA 800 commission reports on aviation security, a number of policy tools have been identified to reduce the likelihood of airplane hijackings. These recommendations often went beyond the obvious cause of the most recent event, suggesting that the recent event did trigger an attempt to improve security. But the historical record also agrees broadly on one key issue: that while aviation security incidents gain a lot of attention in the near term, they have generally not led to the sort of improvements in aviation security that one would expect given their apparent magnitude, as measured by media and congressional attention. These policy tools and the reports that address them are summarized in table 3.2.

When it comes to aviation security, the key questions are: How much security is enough? Who is responsible for providing security? Who pays for it? How do we balance security with increasing demands for air travel? Before September 11, 2001, the aviation security system had not answered these questions. The policy tools that had been developed to secure airplanes from criminal and terrorist attacks are often claimed to provide "defense in depth"; if one system failed to thwart an attack, another would succeed. Systems for isolating potential hijackers through "profiling" systems, x-ray machines, metal detectors, explosives detectors, air marshals, and other methods would serve as layers of protection. The flaw in this thinking is that these systems are not deep defenses—they are broad defenses, designed to provide one layer of protection between a hijacker and a hijacking, on the one hand, or a bomb and the downing of an airplane, on the other.

Agenda Change and Security Incidents

That the three events mentioned above influenced the agenda is well known intuitively, but it is useful to understand the extent to which these events influenced the media, regulatory, and legislative agendas. Figure 3.1 shows how the issue of "aviation security" figured on the agenda of the *New York Times* and the *Congressional Record*. For comparison purposes, the yearly number of news stories or *Congressional Record* entries is indexed to a common base

text continues on p. 73

Table 3.2   Key Issues in Aviation Security since 1985

Passenger screening

Description

Security staff inspects passengers at a security point before boarding to check for weapons, explosives, contraband, or other materials deemed to be a hazard to an aircraft. Debate centers on the training of screeners, high turnover rates, accuracy of searches for weapons, whether screening personnel should be government employees, the performance of screening companies hired by the airlines.

Pan Am 103 Commission Recommendations[a]

That the FAA develop minimum standards for hiring, training, and employing people to perform security functions. Additionally, the FAA should place federal security managers at high-risk airports in the United States and abroad. Those managers would be charged with overseeing the airlines' compliance with security mandates. They would ultimately be responsible for ensuring adequate safety for those traveling on U.S. carriers.

Gore Commission Recommendations

3.2 The FAA should establish federally mandated standards for security enhancements.

3.7 The FAA should work with airlines and airport consortia to ensure that all passengers are positively identified and subjected to security procedures before they board aircraft.

3.10 The FAA should work with industry to develop a national program to increase the professionalism of the aviation security workforce, including screening personnel.

3.20 Certify screening companies and improve screener performance.

3.21 Aggressively test existing security systems.

Marshals

Description

Air marshals are security officials who ride on airplanes and whose presence in the system generally is intended to deter criminal attacks against airliners. Issues surround the numbers of marshals, their cost, and their effectiveness.

Cockpit

Description

The physical security of the cockpit, focusing on the strength of the door and its ability to withstand attempts to open the door and attack the flight crew while in flight.

continued

69

Table 3.2   continued

Arm Crew and/or Provide Security Training

Description

Training of pilots and flight attendants in the use of lethal or nonlethal techniques to subdue and defeat would-be hijackers and bombers. Key issues involve whether pilots should be allowed to carry guns in the cockpit and shoot would-be hijackers, rather than secure the cockpit and land the plane.

Organizational Change

Description

Change in the organizations charged with overseeing aviation security. Involves location of the responsible agency (FAA versus other agency), competence of the organization, new organization versus revamping existing ones.

Pan Am 103 Commission Recommendations

The Commission has recommended that the intelligence and policy functions of the FAA security office be elevated and placed under a new assistant secretary of transportation for security and intelligence. This new assistant secretariat would oversee those operations not just for civil aviation but also for other modes of transportation, such as maritime.

Gore Commission Recommendations

3.12 Establish consortia at all commercial airports to implement enhancements to aviation safety and security.

Explosives

Description

Systems for detecting explosives and explosive devices before they are loaded onto airplanes. Issues surround the workability and cost of the technology, and whether machines, humans, or dogs are most effective.

Pan Am 103 Commission Recommendations

The commission also found major flaws in the FAA's research and development efforts. Too many of those efforts were focused on a technology known as thermal neutron analysis, or TNA. This technology is able to detect some plastic explosives in baggage. However, in addition to operational problems, it has a major limitation—it cannot detect plastic explosives in small quantities that are still large enough to destroy an airliner. Part of the fault for this lies with FAA's approach to developing bomb detection technology—it tried to match a solution with an unclear problem. TNA, as it exists, is a new technology. Its presence implies safety but the level of assurance is slim at best. The com-

Table 3.2 continued

mission has recommended an intensive, accelerated R&D program, with a short-term goal of providing travelers with more than just a sense of security.

Gore Commission Recommendations

3.2 The FAA should establish federally mandated standards for security enhancements.

3.5 The FAA should implement a comprehensive plan to address the threat of explosives and other threat objects in cargo and work with industry to develop new initiatives in this area.

3.18 Significantly expand the use of bomb-sniffing dogs.

3.29 Resolve outstanding issues relating to explosive taggants and require their use.

3.30 Provide regular, comprehensive explosives-detection training programs for foreign, federal, state, and local law enforcement, as well as FAA and airline personnel.

3.31 Create a central clearinghouse within government to provide information on explosives crime.

Bag Match

Description

Ensuring that any bag loaded on an airplane is matched to a passenger who actually boards the plane.

Gore Commission Recommendation

3.24 Begin implementation of full bag–passenger match.

Airport Access Control

Description

Blocking unauthorized personnel from gaining access to secure areas (usually called the landside) of airports.

Gore Commission Recommendation

3.11 Access to airport-controlled areas must be secured and the physical security of aircraft must be ensured.

Passenger Profiling

Description

Using systems such as CAPPSS to develop "profiles," or typical features of would-be hijackers. Concerns arose about the civil liberties implications of these techniques and their effectiveness in preventing criminals and terrorists from boarding planes.

continued

Table 3.2 continued

Gore Commission Recommendation
3.19 Complement technology with automated passenger profiling.

Cargo and Mail
Description
Ensuring that bombs and other hazardous materials are not introduced into the mail or air cargo.

Gore Commission Recommendations
3.3 The U.S. Postal Service should advise customers that all airmail packages weighing more than 16 ounces will be subject to examination for explosives and other threat objects.
3.4 Current law should be amended to clarify the U.S. Customs Service's authority to search outbound international mail.
3.5 The FAA should implement a comprehensive plan to address the threat of explosives and other threat objects in cargo and work with industry to develop new initiatives in this area.

Background Checks
Description
Performing background checks of airport, airline, and screening employees and ensuring that no one with a criminal record is hired to work in a sensitive position.

Gore Commission Recommendations
3.14 Require criminal background checks and FBI fingerprint checks for all screeners and all airport and airline employees with access to secure areas.

General System
Description
All other aspects of the aviation security regime.

Gore Commission Recommendations
3.1 The federal government should consider aviation security a national security issue and provide substantial funding for capital improvements.
3.13 Conduct airport vulnerability assessments and develop action plans.

[a]Summary provided by Senator Frank Lautenberg in the *Congressional Record* (May 15, 1990): S. 2670-71.

by dividing any one year's number of stories in the *Times* or entries in the *Congressional Record* about aviation security by the mean annual number of stories or entries that appeared in these outlets between 1985 and 2002. This allows us to compare the media and Congress on similar scales.

That the September 11 attacks attract the greatest attention in these two domains is unsurprising. The data suggest that Congress tends to react more intensively to an event than the *Times* does, in large part because the agenda space available to Congress for any one issue is considerably more constrained than the space available to the *Times* in covering the issue. This constraint is evidenced by the *Times*'s low but persistent level of coverage of aviation security until the TWA incident versus Congress's almost total inattention to the issue before 1989. Congress, however, became deeply involved in aviation security—among other homeland security aspects—after the September 11 attacks, though its attention, at least among rank-and-file members, declined rapidly after the Aviation and Transportation Security Act (ATSA) was very

Figure 3.1   The Aviation Security Agenda, 1985–2002

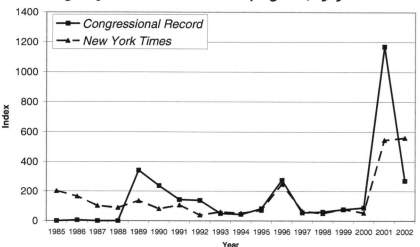

Note: Index is set so that the mean number of *New York Times* and *Congressional Record* entries on the term "aviation security" each year from 1985–2000 is equal to 100.

quickly introduced and enacted in November 2001. A final point of interest is the news media's relatively greater attention to aviation security compared with the congressional agenda in the mid-1980s. Media attention increased during a spate of hijackings and bombings, most of which beset foreign carriers but at least one of which—the hijacking of TWA Flight 847 in 1985—led to considerable news coverage and some congressional committee attention. The Congress as a whole does not appear to have paid much attention to these events in the mid-1980s compared with later events, perhaps because members viewed them as distant or irrelevant to domestic aviation security concerns. Indeed, Americans remained almost smug in their belief that aviation security problems were found overseas more often than in domestic airports.

Let us turn now to the composition of the agenda, with an eye toward discerning learning processes in aviation security. The following two sections consider news media coverage of aviation security to see whether new voices in policy debate are activated by events and whether events correspond with particular policy issues in the domain. I then consider the congressional agenda as measured by the activities of witnesses who testified before congressional committees on the subject of aviation security, in an effort to understand who is mobilized by events and what types of issues arise in response to particular events.

News Coverage of Aviation Security

In this study I analyze stories found on the search term "aviation security" in the *New York Times*. The *Times* thus serves as a proxy for the "well-informed" public agenda. Such a measure is important because media outlets' news judgments about what issues are important may not be precisely the same as policymakers' sense of the key issues. Still, the news media are important conduits of ideas to and from the public and government officials. A review of who is quoted and the ideas that are discussed gives a good sense of what the informed public is thinking about the policy debate that often follows major disasters.

The first question is the extent to which news coverage is primarily driven by an event or other news factors. Only 42 percent of news coverage in the *Times* from 1985 to 2002 was explicitly about any particular event, while the remaining 58 percent was about the issue more broadly. Given the widespread public use of air transportation, its political and utilitarian importance to members of Congress, and the rather spectacular bad outcomes that can result from security breaches, we can say with some confidence that the aviation industry and aviation security are compelling stories for journalists. Of course, as shown in figure 3.1, the most intensive periods of coverage are still connected with particular events, but one cannot say that discussion of aviation security in the *Times* is solely reactive to events.

The high degree of coverage that is not driven by events may be a function of unique features of the *New York Times* on at least two levels. First, the *Times* assigns reporters to the travel and transportation beats. These reporters become experts on these industries, and the aviation industry gains considerable coverage. Other papers are more likely to have general assignment reporters cover these issues, which means less sophisticated coverage, or they merely run wire service copy from sources like the *Times*. Second, the *Times* covers the aviation industry in its business pages rather extensively, as part of a strategy to compete with the *Wall Street Journal* (Raines 2004), which means that beat reporters in particular industries are unlikely to be driven solely by events. The issue is kept alive continuously, at least in the elite media, and we can therefore expect opportunities for debate and discussion of policy alternatives between events, rather than merely in response to them. This continued discussion of the aviation industry in the *Times* reflects how expert journalists become an integral part of the policy community in Paul Sabatier's advocacy coalition framework.

Beyond the substance of news coverage, it is important to consider who is being sought out for information and quoted in news stories. In particular, do events draw new voices into media coverage of aviation security issues? One would expect that if real or apparent security breaches were to influence the agenda, and therefore influence learning, events would activate new voices in the domain or would reorient the most and least dominant voices. This expectation was borne out in the aftermath of the *Exxon Valdez* oil spill, where oil companies and their allies were far less likely to appear at congressional hearings to discuss particular spills than were members of environmental groups and their allies

(Birkland 1997a, chapter 4). In aviation security, one might expect a great outcry from passengers, labor unions, and others with an interest in changing the status quo in security, and we might expect to see less commentary from industry representatives who may wish to maintain the status quo.

Table 3.3 shows the distribution of people quoted in *Times* stories by whether the story was explicitly about a particular aviation security breach. There are several striking features in these data. The first is the degree to which representatives of the federal government dominate discussion of aviation security, regardless of whether an event is on the agenda. Federal sources are even more commonly cited in response to events than in the absence of them, as shown in table 3.4. The most commonly cited government officials when an issue is fresh on the agenda are members of Congress, who often appear to castigate the FAA for its perceived shortcomings in security. Next is the FAA itself, followed by the Department of Transportation (which supervises the FAA), and then the president or his immediate staff, which suggests the importance of this issue, particularly during crises.

Private-sector interests—dominated by the airlines and their trade groups—are also important sources of information. These interests become more important in response to particular events. Labor unions and interest groups are not mobilized by events, and to some extent are demobilized by them, at least in the news. Victims' representatives do get more attention in response to particular events, as do academics and technical experts, but their role in the domain is still small: The bottom line is that between 80 and 98 percent of all stories about aviation security feature government representatives or private-sector interests.

One can hardly say that many voices here are likely to call for improved policy; indeed, there are very few voices from outside the aviation industry. Disaggregating the prevalent subgroups of voices within these dominant groups provides more insight. The two most commonly cited interest group representatives are those from airports (between 40 and 45 percent of all sources within the interest group category) and the Air Transport Association, the trade association for the airlines. Among private-sector voices, the most cited by far are airline officials (50 percent or more of

Table 3.3   Voices Represented in the *New York Times* by Group Type and Agenda Status of Events, 1985–2002

Group Type	Percentage of Stories in Which Group Is Represented		
	Any Event	*No Event*	*Total*
Academics and Experts	3.1	1.0	1.9
Attorneys	0.3	—	0.1
Federal Officials	68.8	54.4	60.5
Foreign Governments	1.0	1.0	1.0
General Public	2.4	0.3	1.2
Interest Groups	9.7	12.7	11.4
Journalists	0.7	0.8	0.7
Local Officials	1.7	2.5	2.2
Other	3.8	4.8	4.4
Pilots	—	0.3	0.1
Political Parties	0.3	—	0.1
Private Individuals	29.5	25.3	27.1
State Officials	1.4	0.3	0.7
Unions	3.8	3.8	3.8
Victims	1.7	0.3	0.9

Note: Sums exceed 100 percent because these are percentages of all stories, which can contain more than one source quotation.

the private-sector voices), with representatives of the screening companies constituting between 25 and 45 percent of sources.

We can conclude from these data that events have very little influence on the types of sources sought out and cited by journalists. One might imagine that aviation security disasters would cause journalists to seek alternative voices or, conversely, that the event would be so striking that groups previously underrepresented in news reports would mount such an aggressive media offensive in the wake of an event that journalists would be compelled to consider their opinions. This is not the case. While passengers and consumers do make up more than half of the individuals categorized under "interest groups," this definition of an interest group is a generous one. Passengers are nowhere near as well organized

Table 3.4 Federal Government Representatives in the *New York Times* by Agency and Agenda Status of Events, 1985–2002

| | Percentage of Stories in Which Group Is Represented | | |
Agency	All Stories	Any Event	No Event
Legislative	37.8	37.4	38.2
Federal Aviation Administration	17.1	15.8	18.2
Department of Transportation	15.9	15.8	16.0
President and Staff	8.2	12.6	4.4
Transportation Security Administration	4.3	1.6	6.7
Department of Justice	3.4	2.6	4.0
Federal Bureau of Investigation	2.4	2.6	2.2
All Others	10.8	11.6	10.2

Note: Sums exceed 100 percent because these are percentages of all stories in which federal officials are quoted, which can have more than one source quotation.

an interest as industry representatives or government agencies. In the end, journalists rely on the same sources regardless of whether a major aviation security breach—or apparent breach—is on the agenda.

This journalistic dependency on experts and officials is probably a function of two facts of aviation security. First, there are very few opposing forces in aviation security and safety. No interest group effectively represents the traveling public's interests. There is one group—the Air Travelers Association—that "lobbies on behalf of airline passenger but, overall, has little clout" (Cobb and Primo 2003, 35). This is due to the widely distributed benefits of any such lobbying effort coupled with the rather focused costs and benefits to the more powerful and influential airline and aviation lobby that derive from favorable regulatory treatment of airlines.

A second reason why there are so few dissenting voices in this domain, and a theme we will see in the case of natural hazards considered in chapter 4, is that aviation policy in general is highly technical and is therefore the province of technical experts who work for the federal government. Peter May argues that such policy domains lack well-defined publics. Policy domains without publics include those that entail "limited development of groups surrounding issues—usually limited to technical and scientific communities." The types of domains that lack publics are those with "public risks and issues with limited incentives for collective action," such as "catastrophic natural and technological hazards" (May 1990, 192).

The result is the application of standard journalistic scripts in airline disasters—whether caused by security failures or other factors, such as mechanical failure. These scripts, which are remarkably familiar in both aviation and natural disasters, are common in crisis news coverage, where, as Conrad Smith (1992) notes, journalists seek to apply news-gathering routines to exceptional events. Cobb and Primo (2003, 6) cite Tuchman's well-known claim that "reports of news events are stories—no more, but no less. . . . Reporters discover events . . . (or are presented with events) in which they can locate themes and conflicts of a particular society. These events get retold as essentially the same story from year to year and from decade to decade" (Tuchman 1978, 23).

The Substance of the Media Agenda

Having established that events are not likely to trigger outside engagement in a closed policy domain, it is worthwhile to ask, does media coverage of events focus on the most obvious causes of the event? Table 3.5 shows the distribution of story subjects by the three major aviation security events, by all other aviation security events, and when no event is mentioned. It is clear that passenger screening generally has dominated this domain, which is unsurprising, as hijacking was always considered an important, if not dominant, mode of attack. Screening is also the aspect of aviation security most visible to most passengers. The dominant theme of each of the three key security events clearly varies. For example, in both the Pan Am and TWA events, the problem of explosives on airplanes dominated the discussion, although there was also considerable discussion of passenger screening in the TWA case, perhaps due to the speculative nature of much of that event's coverage. On the other hand, the high degree of attention paid

Table 3.5 Topics of Stories on Aviation Security, 1985–2002 (percent)

Topics	No Event	All Other Events	1988 Pan Am 103	1996 TWA 800	2001 September 11	Total
Marshal	6	12	1	—	19	7
Screeners, All topics	66	78	61	48	76	67
Screeners, Federalize	17	6	7	4	41	18
Screeners, Wages	4	2	6	4	19	6
Cockpit	3	—	1	—	16	4
Organizational Change	3	—	10	2	6	4
Explosives	17	49	77	54	17	29
Explosives Detection: Machinery	8	18	37	38	9	14
Explosives Detection: Dogs	2	4	4	10	3	3
Positive Baggage Match	5	6	8	31	4	7
Airport Access Control	9	20	13	31	3	11
Perimeter Security	2	12	3	2	2	3
Passenger Profiling	10	16	15	35	13	14
Cargo and Mail	2	4	11	13	—	4
Employee ID	2	4	4	10	2	3
Number of stories	395	49	71	52	116	683

Note: Only topics with 10 percent or more shown. Sums exceed 100 percent because stories can be placed in multiple categories.

to passenger screening in the September 11 attack reflects the failure of the passenger screening system in that event. In essence, we can say that these issues were the key issues in aviation security at the time, and the ones on which professionals in the field focused.

We can conclude thus far that mainstream media coverage of aviation security is dominated by experts, particularly in public-sector agencies, but that, to their credit, the news media focus on the most likely causes of the disaster. The next question is whether Congress is similarly focused, and whether Congress hears from a broader range of voices than those represented in the news media.

Voices and Topics in Congress

While we know that the news media stick to what we might call the expert community in aviation security, does Congress seek to hear a broader spectrum of witnesses in order to learn as much as possible about policy alternatives in aviation security? Table 3.6 shows that it does not. Indeed, the composition of the community testifying before Congress is remarkably similar to that of voices quoted in the news media.

Table 3.6   Testimony on Aviation Security by Witness Affiliation, 1985–2002 (percent)

Witness Affiliation	*Any event on the agenda*	*No event on the agenda*	*All testimony*
Academics and Experts	1.1	2.3	1.7
Attorneys	—	1.1	0.6
Federal Officials	45.0	43.5	44.3
Interest Groups	15.0	16.4	15.7
Private Individuals	33.9	26.6	30.3
State Officials	—	0.6	0.3
Unions	5.0	9.6	7.3
N	*180*	*177*	*357*

Note: Rounded percentages may not sum to be 100%

Table 3.7 Testimony on Aviation Security by Federal Government Witness Affiliation, 1985–2002 (percent)

Witness Affiliation	Any event on the agenda	No event	Total
FAA	24.7	28.6	26.6
Legislative	25.9	20.8	23.4
DOT	9.9	15.6	12.7
Dept. of State	9.9	11.7	10.8
GAO	4.9	7.8	6.3
FBI	7.4	—	3.8
NTSB	6.2	—	3.2
R&D	2.5	3.9	3.2
BATF	1.2	5.2	3.2
N	81	77	158

Note: Only agencies that account for 3 percent or more of testimony are listed here, so percentages may not sum to 100%.

Once again, representatives of the federal government dominate congressional testimony, as befits a domain where regulatory authority rests in the federal government. As shown in table 3.7, the role of individual members of Congress is not as great as it is in media coverage. The FAA dominates testimony whether or not an event is on the agenda, although the FAA and members of Congress are equally prominent when there is an event on the agenda. Events clearly mobilize greater legislative appearances in committees, particularly among nonmembers of committees who are asked to testify because of their expertise or particular interest in an issue. After legislators, the U.S. Department of Transportation (USDOT) is the next most often represented group, again because of its supervisory role over the FAA.

The private sector is the second-most represented block of witnesses. This group is again dominated by the airlines and airport operators, although a large proportion of this testimony is accounted for by representatives of companies that sell explosives-detection and passenger-screening equipment.[3] These witnesses were often called upon by committees to discuss the latest technologies in this field, and they took the opportunity to promote their firms' solutions. This helps explain why more private-sector representatives testify in the wake of an event than in the absence of one. Interest groups were the third-most represented group to appear before Congress, although the figures are somewhat distorted by the dominance of progun advocates, who appeared often, particularly in the 1980s and early 1990s, when concerns were raised over plastic guns that could evade detection at security checkpoints.

Ideas in Congress: Did Dominant Issues Match the "Real" Problem?

While a great deal of attention has been given to a range of issues since the September 11 attacks, it is important to ask a broader question: Did the sorts of problems that emerged as the dominant subject of discussion after Pan Am 103, TWA 800, and September 11 reasonably relate to the putative cause of the accident? The most discussed issues relating to each aviation security event are shown in table 3.8, in which I list all the issues that were discussed by 3 percent or more of the witnesses at aviation security hearings.

The key issues discussed regarding the Pan Am 103 and September 11 disasters are related to the actual likely cause of these incidents. The dominant issue on the agenda after Pan Am 103 was the problem of explosives on airplanes generally, with almost as much discussion of detection technology. Nearly as much attention was paid to problems of security at international airports and international aviation security issues more generally. The shortcomings of passenger screening were the most often cited issue in the aftermath of the September 11 attacks, and this event is the only one that triggered considerable attention to "federalizing" the screening workforce. Somewhat surprisingly, however, attention to explosives on airplanes got nearly as much attention as screening problems did; this focus may be due to the broadening of the entire aviation security debate that followed September 11, discussed below. Both the media and Congress discussed explosives a great deal in the aftermath of TWA 800, which is certainly logical—the loss of TWA 800 looked eerily similar to the destruction of Pan Am 103.

Table 3.8 Topics in Congressional Hearings on Aviation Security, 1985–2002 (percent)

Topics	No event	1988 Pan Am 103	1996 TWA 800	2001 September 11	Total
Screeners	34.1	7.3	9.6	13.6	14.7
Explosives	9.1	15.4	17.5	8.8	11.9
Explosives-Detection Machines	7.7	13.4	16.7	7.0	9.8
Research and Development	8.2	8.5	7.9	3.8	6.5
International Issues	4.1	11.0	3.5	—	5.3
Foreign Airport Security	3.2	11.0	3.5	—	4.9
Screener Training	8.2	3.9	3.5	4.2	4.6
Airport Access Control	1.8	4.4	3.5	4.8	4.0
Passenger Profiling	3.6	1.5	3.5	5.0	3.3
Threats and Notification	—	8.8	—	1.2	3.2
Organizations—Modify	0.9	3.7	0.9	3.8	2.9
Screeners, Federalize	—	—	—	7.4	2.9
Cargo and Mail Security	2.3	1.5	3.5	3.0	2.3
Screening Performance Standards	2.7	2.2	—	3.0	2.3
Cockpit Security	—	—	—	5.4	2.1
Employee Identification Systems	0.5	0.5	—	4.2	1.9
Progress of Investigation	0.9	—	16.7	0.2	1.7
Organizations—Create New	0.5	0.2	—	3.2	1.4

Note: Dashes indicate zero values. Only events and ideas cited by 3 percent or more of witnesses are listed here.

Fewer witnesses testified about TWA 800, however, than about Pan Am 103 or September 11. The TWA 800 investigation moved reasonably quickly to the conclusion that TWA 800 was lost owing to a mechanical failure rather than human intention, even though the FBI continued to seek evidence of terrorism after the fuel tank theory began to dominate professional investigators' theories of the accident (Negroni 2000). Indeed, the "progress of investigations" category was created to reflect the fact that, after it became clear that there was some disagreement between the FBI and the National Transportation Safety Board over the cause of Flight 800's demise, Congress became very interested in the investigation of this particularly troubling incident. In the end, the security issues were largely a restatement of the findings of the Pan Am 103 investigation. It is important to remember, however, that the Gore Commission's mandate related to safety and security, not security alone. This additional emphasis on safety was driven both by the rapidly emerging consensus that the TWA flight was an accident and by another accident, the May 1996 ValuJet crash. Thus, regardless of whether the TWA and ValuJet crashes were caused by security or safety problems, the window of opportunity opened for both of these problems, and the Gore Commission took a comprehensive look at both matters. This is a good example of the kinds of spillover that Kingdon (1995) says will often influence related but not identical domains.

The Breadth of the Agenda:
Do Focusing Events Focus Attention?

As I argued in chapter 1, for learning to occur, preexisting ideas need to be activated or recombined into new ideas. These ideas are debated by participants in a policy domain to advance their preferred problem definition. In *After Disaster* I argued that focusing events create a sharply defined set of issues surrounding an event. Lawrence (2000b), by contrast, in what she calls "event-centered problem definition," argues that events can lead to a remarkable wave of different and often competing causal stories. Much as Hilgartner and Bosk (1988) argue that agenda setting involves the competition of various issues in a particular institutional venue, Regina Lawrence and I (2004) argue that various definitions of the same problem will vie for attention. This is important because the issue itself can gain great attention, and the policy outcomes that result from this attention will usually reflect how the problem and the solutions are constructed.

The central question is this: Does an aviation security event trigger a discussion of a broad or a narrow range of security issues? More specifically, do witnesses focus more closely on the proximate cause of the security breach revealed by a recent event, or does the event cause witnesses to discuss a wide range of aviation security issues? These queries are assessed in table 3.9. A dot is placed in each category if at least one witness discussed the issue. This chart also includes ideas that were enacted into law, which I discuss in the following section. Clearly, the "biggest" event, the September 11 attacks, led to the broadest discussion of aviation security issues, while Pan Am 103 and TWA 800 spawned discussion a narrower range of issues.

Policy Change, Learning, and Implementation

Thus far, this chapter has demonstrated that two aviation security breaches and one suspected breach gained considerable attention, that the substance of that attention can reasonably be related to the most likely cause of these disasters, and that the "bigger" events led to a greater range of issues being discussed because of the event. I also show that the primary voices in the discussion of aviation security come from the private sector and the federal government; airline passengers and the public at large are not deeply involved even though they have obvious interests.

The next question is whether the experience amassed in the United States since 1989 has led to instrumental policy learning. Table 3.8 shows that previous aviation security breaches triggered considerable discussion of issues but many of these issues were not translated into legislative action. This is not to say that nothing happened; there is clear evidence of increased regulatory attention to a wide range of issues. But, as we will see in this section, this regulatory action was widely viewed as a failure.

The data shown in table 3.9 suggest that the one event that has triggered substantial instrumental, social, and policy learning is the September 11 attacks. These attacks triggered considerable congressional testimony about a wide range of issues. As Cobb and Primo note, "There was [after September 11] a marked effect on the aviation industry. Security procedures in the airports and on planes came into question. *All aspects of the security process were reexamined,* severely affecting airline travel. . . . Many policy changes in aviation safety were unprecedented in their scope and in the speed at which they were enacted, *but none of the issues was new to the political agenda*" (2003, 120, emphasis added).

Congress's attention to security after the Pan Am and TWA events was not as comprehensive, and its subsequent lawmaking hewed reasonably closely to what was widely believed to have caused these disasters: bombs in the cargo hold. This assumption was, of course, correct in the Pan Am case though not in the TWA case, but in both incidents concerns about bombs were front and center; concerns about hijacking continued to recede as policymakers believed that this "old" problem had been rectified.

We can say, then, that there is evidence of instrumental learning about a limited range of aviation security matters after Pan Am 103 and TWA 800. There is less evidence, however, of social policy or political learning after these events. Rather, policymakers believed that these events were simply further manifestations of what they already believed to be true: Bombs would be the major terrorist threat to commercial aviation in the future. Hijacking was not perceived as an important hazard. In other words, the social construction of the terrorist problem and the understanding of the causes and consequences of terrorism directed against aviation did not appreciably change after these events.

This lack of learning does not mean that the importance of these events in the overall history of attempts to protect commercial aviation from terrorism was not appreciated. It is entirely possible that without the experience gleaned from these two events, legislators and key executive branch leaders would not have had the rich body of ideas available immediately after September 11. The Pan Am and TWA events provided two kinds of information that policymakers could draw on after September 11. The first was the fruit of two presidential commissions formed to

Table 3.9 Ideas Contained in Congressional Testimony and Legislation on Aviation Security, 1988–2002

Policy	No event mentioned	1988 Pan Am 103	PL 101-604, Aviation Security Improvement Act of 1990	1996 TWA 800	PL 104-264, FAA Auth. Act of 1996	PL 106-181, FAA Auth. Act (1999)	PL 106-528, Airport Security Improvement Act of 2000	2001 Sept. 11	PL 107-71, Aviation and Transportation Security Act (2001)	PL 107-296, Homeland Security Act of 2002
Air Marshals		•						•	•	
Airport Perimeter Security	•	•						•		
Airport Access Control	•	•	•	•				•	•	
Cargo and Mail Security	•	•	•	•	•			•	•	
Cockpit Security	•							•	•	
Employee Background Checks	•	•	•	•	•		•	•	•	
Employee Identification Systems	•	•						•	•	
Explosives and Explosives Detection	•	•		•	•	•		•	•	•
Foreign Airport Security	•	•		•						
Organizations—Modify or Create	•	•						•	•	•
Passenger Profiling	•	•		•	•			•	•	

Pilots—Arms, Fatal	•	•	•					
Pilots—Arms, Non-fatal		•	•					
Positive Bag Match		•	•	•	•	•	•	•
Research and Development			•		•		•	•
Screeners—General, Training, Compensation		•	•		•	•	•	•
Screeners—Certification of Screening Companies			•		•	•		•
Screeners—Federalize			•					
Screeners—Require Screeners be Citizens	•		•					
Screeners—Subject Airline Employees to Checkpoint Screening		•	•				•	•
Screeners—Screening Company Performance Standards							•	•
Security Training—Pilots and Crew		•	•				•	•

Note: Shaded cells indicate that ideas present in testimony about the event were also reflected in legislation related to the event.

investigate these security breaches and to provide recommendations. The second was the accumulation of reports, mostly from the General Accounting Office (GAO), that detailed ongoing shortcomings in security policy.[4]

Presidential Commissions on Aviation Security

After the crash of Pan Am 103, Senator Frank Lautenberg (D-NJ) led other senators in introducing a resolution (S. Res. 86, March 17, 1989) that asked the president "to appoint a special commission to consider the destruction of Pan American World Airways Flight 103, and the security of air travel." While the Bush administration initially resisted the establishment of a commission on national security grounds, citing its belief that existing investigations by the FAA and other authorities would be sufficient, the administration ultimately relented. The Presidential Commission on Aviation Security and Terrorism was created by Executive Order 12686 on August 4, 1989, and presented its report on May 15, 1990. Its chair, Ann McLaughlin, a former labor secretary in the Reagan administration, testified before Congress once after the commission's work was complete, but there is no evidence of repeat appearances before Congress. The commission generated a series of recommendations involving security procedures and in particular the detection of explosives. Many of these recommendations were gathered into a bill, the Aviation Security Improvement Act of 1990, PL 101-604 (November 16, 1990). At the same time that the commission was investigating aviation security, Congress held seven hearings directly on the aviation security issue between February 9 and September 27, 1990.

The creation of a commission to investigate the crash of TWA 800 was somewhat less contentious. On August 22, 1996, on his own initiative, President Clinton created the White House Commission on Aviation Safety and Security, headed by Vice President Al Gore, which submitted its final report on February 12, 1997. This commission was presumably a high priority for the administration, given its high-profile leadership. However, as seen in the resulting legislation—the Federal Aviation Authorization Act of 1996, PL 104-264—the Gore Commission largely repeated the same calls for change in addressing explosives and general system safety issues that had been raised after Pan Am 103. At least sixteen hearings were held on PL 104-264; many of the hearings focused on the aviation system, including air traffic control and safety, but the implementation of the recommended changes was remarkably slow.

The similarities between the two commissions are striking. Both were created for three reasons. First, Congress did not believe it had the information it needed in order to act. Second, there was no particular sense of urgency driving immediate change, which allowed Congress the luxury of delegating the issue to a study commission. Third, these commissions were somewhat less partisan and more reliable than congressional committees. Once the commissions met and issued their recommendations, however, the urge to act had largely passed. While Congress passed legislation to implement their recommendations, the legislation and the promulgated regulations were largely ineffective, as demonstrated in a series of reports discussed below.

The GAO Reports on Aviation Security

Between 1987 and 2003 the General Accounting Office (GAO) issued fifty-two reports on various aspects of aviation security, most of them addressing the key aspects of aviation security discussed in this book and particularly emphasizing screeners and explosives detection. The authors of these reports made an effort to recognize FAA efforts to improve security, but the efforts made in the 1990s were generally weak and ineffective, and congressional mandates were largely ignored, leading the GAO to issue reports with startlingly clear titles: *Aviation Security: Corrective Actions Under Way But Better Inspection Guidance Still Needed* (1988); *Aviation Safety and Security: Challenges to Implementing the Recommendations of the White House Commission on Aviation Safety and Security* (1997); *Aviation Security: Implementation of Recommendations Is Under Way, But Completion Will Take Several Years* (1998); *Aviation Security: Slow Progress in Addressing Long-Standing Screener Performance Problems* (2000); *Aviation Security: Vulnerabilities Still Exist in the Aviation Security System* (2000); and *Aviation Security:*

Terrorist Acts Illustrate Severe Weaknesses in Aviation Security (September 2001).

These reports highlighted the failure of the FAA and other responsible parties to implement recommended changes. In a 1998 report, for example, the GAO found that of three recommendations made in the Gore Commission report, only one, relating to sharing of intelligence information, had been implemented by 1997, while one had been partially implemented and the third was nowhere near implementation. Moreover, the GAO found that the "FAA has made progress but encountered delays in implementing the five recommendations made by the Commission and the similar mandates contained in the Reauthorization Act. These delays have occurred in large part because the recommendations involve new technologies and, in some cases, require FAA to issue regulations" (U.S. GAO 1988b). The last point is important: Recent aviation security policy often rested on the belief that the passage of legislation would spur the rapid adoption of new technology. However, the deployment of explosives-detection technology has been more costly, controversial, and technically difficult than lawmakers envisioned, and this aspect of aviation security has stalled as a result.

The GAO's claim that policy change is slow because of the time it takes the FAA to issue regulations is curious at best. Making rules is admittedly time consuming, given public comment and other "sunshine" requirements. But is delay necessarily related to procedural requirements? Or is it the result of conflict between interests that occurs in implementation and drags out the process, in the form of such things as extensions of time for final comments? I do not address this question directly here, but the FAA's long history of delays, false starts, and outright failures to act— all documented by the GAO—suggests that something more fundamental than the usual slow pace of regulatory change is at work here. Rather, it appears that the FAA has been more solicitous of industry opinion than some advocates would argue is desirable. One might argue that this concern benefits from perfect hindsight, but this issue was raised by the GAO, members of Congress, enterprising journalists, and bureaucratic whistle-blowers long before September 11, 2001.

Summarizing Post–September 11 Learning

The recommendations of the Pan Am and TWA commissions were not, the GAO found, quickly or effectively put into practice. These recommendations and the limited statutory and regulatory change they spawned were available to policymakers immediately after September 11, which explains why there was no need for a new commission to study possible policy changes after the terrorist attacks. The September 11 attacks highlighted the very things the commissions and the GAO had been saying about aviation safety and led to the remarkably rapid enactment of the ATSA. This bill was introduced on September 21, 2001, as S. 1447 and was enacted into law a mere fifty-nine days later, on November 19, 2001. The process was so quick that only five hearings were held on the issue, and much of their substance was repetitive.

Table 3.10 summarizes the types of learning in aviation security and suggests that learning occurred after all three major events, but September 11 is clearly the event that triggered the most learning and the most change. Instrumental learning is quite clear after September 11: It was clear that a primary policy tool—security screening by private contractors—had failed, and the result was four hijackings in a single day. But September 11 revealed more than a single policy failure. Social learning was enhanced by knowledge that hijackers are likely to be suicidal and fanatical, and not "rational" in the way that we previously believed a "rational" hijacker should or would act. This change in our understanding of what terrorists are capable of doing has led to considerable change in how we view the potential outcomes of airplane hijackings. Political actors learned that they could use the September 11 attacks as the ultimate example of the consequences of failure to learn from events. If we cannot cause change after so horrible a disaster, the argument goes, what will it take?

While this social and political learning largely occurred after September 11, it is important to remember that instrumental learning was happening throughout the 1990s and beyond. The difference between the September 11 attacks and the other events was the spectacular nature of the event, the willingness of the relevant agencies (such as the FAA) to act quickly to implement changes, and the breadth of the resulting changes. But these

Table 3.10 Evidence of Learning in Aviation Security

		Policy Learning				
	Instrumental	Evidence of Instrumental Learning	Social	Evidence of Social Learning	Political	Evidence of Political Learning
Requisite Conditions	Improved understanding of policy instruments or implementation based on experience or formal evaluation.	Accumulation of knowledge about implementation failure based on the results of attacks.	Improved understanding or alteration of dominant causal beliefs about a policy problem or solution within the relevant policy domain.	Accumulation of information about terrorist attacks on airliners.	Awareness of political prospects and factors that affect them.	Aviation interests learned that change was inevitable after September 11; strategy shifted to making these changes economically acceptable.

Prima Facie Indicators	Policy redesign entailing change in instruments for carrying out the policy, e.g., inducements, penalties, assistance, funding, timing of implementation, organizational structures.	Changes in policy foci in response to recent threats. Examples: Explosives detection in Pan Am 103 and TWA 800; attention to screeners and screening after September 11.	Policy redefinition entailing change in policy goals or scope, e.g., policy direction, target groups, rights bestowed by the policy.	Learning that ultimate target of policy is terrorists, not hijacking for transportation or ransom. Redefinition of hijackings from a transportation problem to a national security problem.	Policy advocates change in political strategy, e.g., shifting arenas, offering new arguments, employing new tactics for calling attention to a problem or idea.	Shift in tactics from opposition to security to support for security coupled with aid to airlines.
Evidence required	Increased understanding of policy instruments or implementation.	Expert demands for change, presidential commissions, and legislative change encompassing some of these recommendations, all with an eye toward policy refinement.	Change in dominant causal beliefs within the relevant policy domain.	Evidence of change in attitudes toward hijackers as likely to be terrorists; terrorists now assumed to be potentially suicidal.	Awareness of relationship between political strategy and political feasibility within a given advocacy coalition.	Evidence of awareness that the previous arguments would be hard to defend.

Source: Modified from May (1992).

changes also raise an important question: Has a lesson really been learned if it is not implemented?

Implementation Problems in Aviation Security

Students of the policy process have found that the implementation stage is often where attention drops off and problems arise that diminish the high hopes that accompany the passage of legislation (Nice and Grosse 2001, 57). The passage of legislation often removes an issue from the immediate congressional agenda, and journalists pay less attention as an issue moves from front-page headlines to the more mundane realm of daily administration. There are many examples of legislators and executives with excessively high expectations, in terms of both management techniques and the application of technology. It is also very common that funding and other resources fail to match the perceived needs addressed by the legislation. In addition, once legislation is passed and reaches the implementation stage, conflict between the parties most directly influenced by it often tends to increase.

Given that Congress's oversight of the FAA is generally "fire-alarm" oversight, triggered only by the very sorts of disasters described in this book, it is unsurprising that the lessons of Pan Am 103 and TWA 800 (to the extent those events caused instrumental learning) were largely forgotten. As memories of these disasters faded, Congress shifted its attention away from security and toward safety and consumer convenience.

There are two ways in which we can explain why aviation security efforts did not meet the expectations of legislative drafters in the 1990s, and why the implementation of post–September 11 changes will be challenging. First, implementation of policy changes will become more difficult as the low-hanging fruit is picked. The low-hanging fruit in the ATSA include much more stringent passenger screening, inspection of luggage, more restrictions on the sorts of things that can be carried aboard aircraft, and in particular the "federalization" of the passenger-screening workforce to ensure that weapons are detected. Screening changes in particular, including the deployment of Transportation Security Administration (TSA) screeners, were accomplished quickly because they were very symbolically important measures designed to add some measure of security and at the same time reassure the traveling public that *something* was being done. The urge to do *something, anything*, is often quite strong after focusing events (Nice and Grosse 2001).

While many of the screening processes and training for screeners were improved shortly after the enactment of ATSA, Kenneth Mead, the inspector general of the USDOT, noted in January 2002 that "while progress has been made, clearly the heavy lifting (installing explosives-detection systems to screen all checked baggage and hiring a workforce) lies ahead" (Mead 2002). In particular, machinery for detecting explosives was not installed rapidly after passage of ATSA, owing to technological and practical considerations: The machines were quite large, and airports were not designed to accommodate them. Meanwhile, even the implementation of the "easy" parts of aviation security came in for significant criticism and questioning in 2005, perhaps suggesting some sort of fatigue with the cost and the inconvenience of the new security regime. This waxing and waning is an example of the "issue-attention cycle" (Downs 1972), in which an event triggers enthusiastic calls for policy change that are then muted as the costs of change are weighed against the likelihood that an event will recur.

Second, conflict will arise over implementation even when a dramatic event creates great pressure for some sort of change. One might assume that the September 11 attacks were so momentous that the aviation industry would find it difficult to oppose any proposed policy change. Opposition might even be seen as heartless or unpatriotic. This may be the case in the most visible areas of aviation security, such as passenger screening and explosives detection, where measures to address the issue had to be taken quickly for both substantive and symbolic reasons. But the less obvious aspects of the lessons of September 11 are still prone to debate and disagreement. There has been debate over whether the transponders on airplanes should be able, with one quick action by a member of the flight crew, to transmit a signal to air traffic control (ATC) that the plane has been hijacked. A transponder is a radio device that transmits the plane's flight number, position, speed, and altitude to ATC, so that controllers need not rely solely on the radar "echo" produced by ATC's radar transmitters.

Under international rules, crew members set transponders to transmit code 7500 to signal that the plane has been hijacked. The intent of the FAA's proposed transponder rules is to make it easier for crews to indicate that they are being hijacked and to ensure that transponders transmit continuously (and are not shut off, as they were on the four September 11 flights), thereby alerting controllers that there is a problem onboard the plane. This immediate and constant signal would give relevant authorities time to respond to the hijacking. In the post–September 11 environment, one option would be to shoot down a hijacked plane if the hijackers appeared to intend to convert the plane into a guided missile. The FAA has taken initial steps to require the continuous operation of a transponder broadcasting the 7500 code and to make it impossible for a hijacker to turn off the transponder. However, as of mid-2005, the issue had not been settled (Ramsey 2005).

The Air Transport Association—an interest group representing the major U.S. air carriers—opposes changes to the transponder rules on the grounds that these measures are "too costly," would be ineffective, and that the cost burden properly belongs to the federal government, not the airline industry (Bond 2003). One cannot simply dismiss this as yet another example of industry resistance to security measures. An argument can be made that in the history of aviation, security cost considerations have been at least equal to, if not more important than, security effectiveness. In the transponder case, however, the arguments against continuous transponder operation may be compelling. These arguments include cost, the possibility of false alarms with no way to rescind the false alarm, and the fact that such a rule may not be necessary, since already enacted requirements regarding cockpit door strength and ground screening of passengers may prevent anyone from doing something untoward on the plane in the first place (Learmount 2003). In essence, one can argue that the transponder change is more difficult to make than the other, more obvious changes, in part because this particular problem was identified more recently than the more familiar problems of securing airports and airplanes were. Thus experience with any sort of "transponder problem" has failed to accumulate.

The failure to implement other key aviation security measures is well documented in the news media and in GAO reports. The

FAA did not fully implement existing requirements that explosive detection devices be installed and used at airports. And perhaps most important after September 11, it became clear that FAA efforts to certify the companies that screened passengers before boarding were entirely ineffective. The FAA was on the verge of issuing a rule on the certification of screening companies before the September 11 attacks overtook this process. To be fair, the FAA did react very quickly to the September 11 attacks, banning and screening for a great many more potential weapons than before and requiring that security companies be much more careful in their screening in the months between September 11 and the assumption of aviation security duties by the TSA. In essence, September 11 sped up FAA efforts to implement existing laws and regulations, but the agency's foot-dragging before September 11 meant that many of these functions would be taken away from the agency. The events of September 11 were so overwhelming that they called for immediate action, and Congress believed that the FAA was not up to the task.

Finally, as noted earlier, the passage of time will reduce enthusiasm for some policy changes that seemed entirely sensible when they were first enacted; this decline in enthusiasm will influence implementation outcomes. By 2005, for example, significant questions had been raised about whether federal screeners were doing any better at detecting weapons and other dangerous items than the private screeners they replaced had been. Much of this criticism was driven by weariness with the long lines and seemingly random nature of airport checkpoint searches. The media have reported many stories of screeners who failed to detect a weapon and of searches of grandmothers, children, congressional representatives, and others who pose no threat to aviation. As the memory of September 11 fades, the possibility of relaxing security measures increases, particularly as the number of complaints about screening increases.

Conclusions

The policymaking outcomes of September 11 suggest that the aviation security domain had a repository of ideas and potential policy responses developed after earlier security and safety incidents that, in retrospect, only needed a focusing event to spur action. Clearly, learning in this domain was cumulative. While all who participate in policymaking in the domain decry the reactive nature of policy-making in aviation security, it is also true that after September 11 there was no need to reinvent the wheel. There was a wealth of ideas from which to draw, as reflected in the broad scope of changes enacted in the Aviation and Transportation Security Act and the Homeland Security Act.

While September 11 created sweeping change in aviation security policy, these changes were made possible by a rich history of efforts to improve policy, and a history of incremental policy that in some ways improved security and in other ways failed to do so. There is considerable evidence of learning in this domain, but there is also a history of failures to *apply* the lessons of aviation security breaches for very long after the event. The key exception to this cycle of learning lessons without implementation may be the September 11 attacks, which led to a much more stringent review and reorganization of both the tools and the agencies charged with aviation security. Even today, more than five years after the event, weariness with new security procedures, coupled with apparently endless well-publicized breaches of security and failures in the passenger screening process, suggest that the post–September 11 period may look more like the pre–September 11 era than one might have originally assumed.

In the aviation policy domain, it is abundantly clear that there is little or no interest in group mobilization, in large part because there are few if any interest groups that could be mobilized to press for effective aviation security measures. This is due in large part to the nature of air travel as a commodity. In such a policy domain, the providers of the good are much more likely than its consumers to organize to protect their interests. There are few incentives to form an interest group representing airline passengers, but many to form industry groups. Indeed, this is a classic collective action problem (Olson 1971), in which incentives for organization tilt in favor of interests with an economic stake in policy. That said, we do not see much event-related mobilization of any groups (apart from representatives of private firms that sell technologies such as scanning machinery) that could prevent guns or bombs from getting onto airplanes. Apart from these private companies, the group nature of policymaking in this domain does not change much when an event is fresh on the agenda. What changes is the mobilization of particular ideas in the domain, and September 11 triggered discussion of a particularly wide range of issues in this domain.

The aviation security domain shows considerable prima facie evidence of instrumental and social learning from the September 11 attacks and lesser evidence of learning after earlier attacks. Evidence of instrumental learning most clearly includes the substantive policy changes that have followed the major aviation security incidents from 1985 to 2001. These include changes to policy instruments designed to address more clearly emerging threats from explosives, and, after September 11, flaws in passenger screening systems. Evidence of social policy learning includes the shift from treating aviation security as the domain of the transportation sector to seeing it as a national security problem with national consequences for policy design and implementation. Even if, in the end, aviation security concerns move away from the national security concerns raised immediately after September 11, one can discern a shift from treating aviation security as a private good to be paid for and enjoyed only by the traveling public and the airlines to one paid for and enjoyed by all Americans. As we learned after September 11, one need not be on board an airplane to be the victim of a hijacking.

Political learning also took place after the event, as the airline industry learned very quickly that it would be unable to oppose major overhauls of aviation security policy and would have to seek a compromise in an environment that was very much biased in the direction of policy change. As noted above, however, future research is needed if we are to fully understand the motivations of those involved in making political arguments for or against various policy changes relating to aviation security.

The evidence presented here strongly suggests that post–September 11 policy is in part a product of all the experience with aviation security that had been amassed before the attacks. This raises an important question that deserves greater attention in studies of policy learning: whether we can say that instrumental learning really has happened if the policy instruments enacted by

Congress are not fully implemented by responsible regulators. There is clearly a gap between instrumental policy learning and the implementation of policy tools. The literature and research on implementation may well provide some insights into why lessons are learned but not applied.

four

learning from earthquakes and hurricanes

This chapter reviews how policies intended to mitigate earth-quakes and hurricanes have shown some evidence of learning over the long run. Two particularly interesting findings emerge from the research. First, learning to mitigate natural disasters is incremental and is not particularly salient to a broad range of public officials whose interests lie more in the provision of disaster relief than in mitigation. Learning about mitigation in the wake of a disaster has taken a back seat to the provision of immediate disaster relief. Indeed, the desire to recover quickly from natural disasters may be the biggest impediment to mitigation. Disasters do not lead directly to new policies in the same way that aviation security events trigger relatively rapid change. Second, there are major differences in event-related learning in earthquakes and hurricanes, and these differences are a direct result of the social and political organization of the policy communities that address these hazards.

Much disaster research tends to take a deeply normative tone. In the natural hazards domain, we find considerable evidence of what "should" be learned both in response to disasters and in periods of "normal" politics. Expert opinion on what should be done is likely to provide a benchmark for assessing whether the sort of policy change sought by experts actually occurs. This is particularly important because, as I found in *After Disaster* (1997), there is no more than one advocacy coalition that promotes improved natural hazards policies based on its sense of the public interest (Sabatier and Jenkins-Smith 1993).

After considering to what extent there has been disaster-related learning at the federal level, I turn to a discussion of state-level learning from earthquakes in California and Washington and hurricanes in Florida and North Carolina. This analysis shows that disaster-related learning and policy change can occur at the state as well as the national level. The local dimension is much more important when dealing with natural disasters than in the matter of aviation security for the simple reason that the federal government has legal responsibility for aviation, while state and local governments have the greatest influence over policy tools in the realm of natural disasters. Indeed, most federal disaster mitigation policy is designed to induce state and local governments to take action. The federal government does not and cannot impose many mitigation techniques directly on local communities.

Why Natural Hazards Matter

People throughout the United States live in areas that are exposed to a wide array of hazards, including earthquakes, hurricanes, floods, windstorms, tornadoes, landslides, wildfires, tsunamis, volcanic eruptions, and so on. The distribution of these hazards is not uniform—the earthquake hazard is higher in California than in Kansas, for example—but it is fair to say that a substantial amount of the land area of the United States is at risk for one or more natural hazards.

Disasters are socially constructed; a natural phenomenon is perceived as a disaster only if it hurts people. As we will see later in this chapter, hazards (the potential for a disaster) and disasters are not merely physical properties or immutable scientific facts. Whether a hazard exists or a disaster has occurred is as much a social and political question as it is a scientific one (Stallings 1995).

People suffer from natural hazards through physical injury or death or through loss of property. Property damage can hurt individuals directly when one's house is flooded or burned out, or indirectly, as when critical infrastructure such as roads, transit, water, sewer, power, and telecommunications is lost. Because these services are so important, they are known as "lifelines." Damage to lifelines can be as disruptive to people as damage they might experience at home, or more so. For example, many houses survived the 1994 Northridge and 1989 Loma Prieta earthquakes in California with little damage, yet people in the Los Angeles and San Francisco areas were greatly inconvenienced when roads were closed and utilities were cut.

The economic impact of natural disasters is greater than mere inconvenience. While the number of deaths from individual disasters in the United States is declining, the economic toll they take is large and growing. Natural disasters cause about $20 billion each year in direct damage and $30 to $35 billion in indirect damage. Just two disasters, Hurricane Hugo and the Loma Prieta earthquake, did more than $15 billion in direct damage. In 2004 Hurricanes Charley and Frances did a combined total of $5 to $10 billion in damage in Florida, although such figures are always variable and hard to fix precisely. Hurricane Katrina may be the largest natural disaster in dollar terms in U.S. history, with damage exceeding $50 billion.

Hurricane winds do considerable damage, but the storm surge, the wall of water propelled by wind and waves, also damages the shoreline. Hurricanes tend to strike most often in the southeastern United States. States at greatest risk are the Carolinas, Georgia, Florida, Alabama, Mississippi, Louisiana, and Texas, but the storms can move up the coast and affect northern states as well. Improvements in building and in planning and hazard reduction programs are largely offset each year by the increasing number of people and the increasing value of property in high-risk areas (Burby and Dalton 1993, 229; National Research Council 1991).

Most people associate the earthquake hazard with California, but at least thirty-nine states are subject to earthquakes (FEMA 1992). Earthquakes have struck Massachusetts in the 1700s, Charleston, South Carolina, in 1889, south-central Alaska in 1964, and the Puget Sound region of Washington State in 1948, 1965, and 2001. Future earthquakes of the scale that struck near New Madrid, Missouri, in 1811 and 1812 could do substantial damage to the St. Louis and

Memphis areas. While the threat of earthquakes in areas outside California is known to professionals in this field, public appreciation of the threat outside California is considerably lower.

Disaster Mitigation as a Primary Goal of Disaster Policy

Because of the potential for substantial injury, loss of life, and economic disruption and property loss, many engineers, social scientists, policy analysts, and practitioners believe that more should be done both to raise awareness of disaster mitigation and to promote its practice. Mitigation is any action that would lessen the impact of a natural disaster. Research on mitigation emphasizes a preference for policies that employ land-use controls, improved building codes, or actuarially sound insurance programs. Other policy alternatives, such as building levees, dams, breakwaters, and groins and replenishing beach sand, tend to be short-term palliatives rather than long-term solutions. Indeed, these techniques tend to ignore what has been learned through scientific, social scientific, and behavioral research, but often provide a "false sense of security" that mitigation is a large-scale government effort and will work even in the face of catastrophic events. A selected list of key hazards legislation, including legislation that promotes mitigation, is shown in table 4.1.

Promoting mitigation is challenging in part because it is a relatively new aspect of disaster policy, although research has long promoted mitigation as a means of protecting lives and property. Federal efforts to alleviate suffering in the wake of disasters have traditionally concentrated on disaster relief after the fact, not on mitigation in advance. The Disaster Relief Act of 1950 (PL 81-875) was considered an important improvement because it created a general disaster relief law that replaced ad hoc, event-specific aid packages. Subsequent legislation has often been event specific and, as is typical of distributive policy, is characterized by logrolling and a focus on the needs of particular areas. May (1985, 21) notes that such logrolling was not only predicated on potential future disasters but also based on past disasters. Aid provisions retroactive to prior disasters have often been written into new relief measures to ensure broader support, but mitigation has received little or no attention. Platt (1999) notes that disaster declarations are profoundly political in that they provide the executive branch and Congress with opportunities to distribute federal aid. This was particularly true during the Clinton administration, which learned from FEMA's mishandling of Hurricane Andrew in 1992 that rapid delivery of relief pays substantial political dividends.

Federal policy does not ignore mitigation completely, and in recent years it has become more prominent. Perhaps the earliest and still the best-known mitigation program is the National Flood Insurance Program, which requires that communities adopt building and planning standards in floodplains before property owners are allowed to purchase federally subsidized flood insurance. This is a powerful incentive to engage in mitigation, as holders of federally backed mortgages are required to purchase flood insurance for property in defined flood hazard areas. But this type of mitigation has often been ineffective in reducing damage. While it has encouraged some mitigation in the way structures are built, flood insurance premiums are not based on a property's risk profile. Rather, premiums are set artificially low, thereby creating what insurance professionals call a "moral hazard"—that is, a hazard created when insurance makes people take greater risks than they would without insurance. Artificially low flood insurance rates have subsidized real estate development in flood-prone areas where development should be discouraged. The Flood Insurance Reform Act of 2004 (PL 108-264) may reduce this subsidy somewhat for property owners in flood-prone areas in a way that may well increase efforts to mitigate flood damage. This law was designed to require more aggressive mitigation measures, including improved land-use practices, among other things.

The National Earthquake Hazards Reduction Act of 1977, which created the National Earthquake Hazards Reduction Program (NEHRP), promoted research to mitigate hazards (including, on first enactment, a program to attempt to predict earthquakes). But this program is plagued by the usual gap between knowledge and actual policy, particularly outside California, where there is little planning at the state level and where building codes are usually not promulgated with earthquakes in mind.

Table 4.1 Selected Legislation on Natural Hazards, 1950–2004

Year	Legislation	Summary
1950	Disaster Relief Act of 1950, PL 81-875	Formalized existing practice allowing for funding to repair local public facilities.
1956	Federal Flood Insurance Act, PL 84-1016	Flood insurance program that never started because the House rejected funding for it.
1966	Disaster Relief Act of 1966, PL 89-769	Amended 1950 act to allow rural communities to participate; aid for damaged higher education facilities; repair of public facilities under construction.
1968	National Flood Insurance Act of 1968, PL 90-448	First flood insurance program, enacted as Title VIII of the Housing and Development Act.
1969	Disaster Relief Act of 1969, PL 91-79	Debris removal, food aid, unemployment benefits, loan programs revised; duration limited to fifteen months.
1970	Disaster Assistance Act of 1970, PL 91-606	Continues most provisions of the 1969 law, plus grants for temporary housing or relocation, funding for legal services.
1973	Flood Disaster Protection Act of 1973, PL 93-234	Expanded coverage, imposed sanctions on communities in flood zones that failed to participate in flood insurance.

Year	Act	Description
1974	Disaster Relief Amendments of 1974, PL 93-288	Defined "major disasters" and "emergencies," broadened categories of allowable expenditures. Served as template for most policy until the Stafford Act. In 1977 this act was reauthorized through 1980 (PL 95-51). Again reauthorized in 1980 (PL 96-568).
1977	National Earthquake Hazards Reduction Act, PL 95-124	Bill enacted to address concerns raised by Alaska and San Fernando earthquakes, among other events. Included provisions to support research on prediction and mitigation.
1988	Robert T. Stafford Disaster Relief and Emergency Assistance Act, PL 100-707	Amended Disaster Relief Amendments of 1974. Increased emphasis on mitigation.
1993	Stafford Act Amendments, 103-181	Enhanced 1988 law to emphasize mitigation.
2000	Disaster Mitigation Act, PL 106-390	Encouraged state and local hazard mitigation, required enhanced state and local mitigation planning.
2002	Homeland Security Act, PL 107-296	Made FEMA a part of the new Department of Homeland Security.
2004	Flood Insurance Reform Act of 2004, PL 108-264	Provisions to encourage owners of repeatedly flooded properties to accept buyouts or lose eligibility for flood insurance.
2004	National Windstorm Impact Reduction Act of 2004, Title II of PL 108-360	Created a National Windstorm Impact Reduction Program patterned after the earthquake program. This law is part of the earthquake program reauthorization.

Source: Based on May (1985), tables 2.2, 2.3, and 2.4.

Mitigation has traditionally received less attention than other aspects of disasters because of the routine pressures on government officials and citizens to deal with problems that are much more salient until there is a disaster (May 1985, 8; Rossi, Wright, and Weber-Burdin 1982). Once a disaster strikes, local officials and residents focus on relief and reconstruction and pay little attention to the next possible disaster. Of course, the rebuilding process is the best time for implementing mitigation measures, but paradoxically this is when mitigation tends to receive the least attention. Once reconstruction is under way, people tend to lose interest in mitigation, leaving technical experts to attempt, with varying levels of success, to keep the issue on the agenda. Their challenge is compounded by the absence of a social movement galvanized by the threat of natural disasters (Stallings 1995), making natural hazards policy a "policy without publics" (May 1990).

From the federal and perhaps also the state perspective, mitigation is a problem of local implementation. Intergovernmental policy implementation can be particularly challenging, especially when the national government fails to pressure local officials to keep mitigation on the agenda (Goggin et al. 1990). Once the immediate crisis has passed and communities return to something approaching "normalcy," the community moves on to other issues (Alesch and Petak 1986; Prater and Lindell 2000; Rossi, Wright, and Weber-Burdin 1982). Mitigation therefore fails to gain the attention that proponents of disaster policy would like to see. Indeed, this phenomenon is behind the federal government's requirements for state mitigation plans under the Stafford Act and for more stringent state and local mitigation planning under the Disaster Mitigation Act of 2000. The latter act reduces the availability of federal mitigation funds to jurisdictions that fail to do mitigation planning. One wonders, of course, how effective such a threat can be if local interest in mitigation is low at the outset. In short, interest in mitigation is institutionalized in the community of professionals who deal with disasters, but not more broadly in state and local government.

FEMA's shift away from preparedness for nuclear war and toward natural hazards relief and mitigation (Kreps 1990) was foreshadowed by the enactment of the Robert T. Stafford Disaster Relief and Emergency Assistance Act of 1988. Before the Stafford

Act (which was further strengthened by the Disaster Mitigation Act of 2000), very little attention was paid to hazard mitigation across all hazards. The term is mentioned favorably a few times in the Disaster Relief Act of 1974, but mitigation took a back seat to efforts to organize federal disaster relief agencies. These efforts culminated in 1979 with the creation, through a reorganization plan, of the Federal Emergency Management Agency. Once FEMA was created, its effectiveness and sense of mission as an agency were not located firmly in natural hazards broadly or in mitigation in particular until James Lee Witt, former director of emergency management for Arkansas, was appointed FEMA director by President Clinton in 1993.

This is not to say that mitigation was solely Witt's idea; the original Stafford Act predated his arrival at FEMA and provided a new program for hazard mitigation under section 404. For mitigation projects, this section allowed the federal government to allocate a sum equal to 10 percent of federal moneys granted to states on "repair and restoration of facilities" following disasters (section 406). The mitigation funds, under a program called the Hazard Mitigation Grant Program (HMGP), went to states only if they had prepared a mitigation plan under section 409. Section 409 has since been repealed, replaced by a new planning regime under section 322 of the Disaster Management Act of 2000, in large part because there was little relationship between mitigation planning and actual mitigation projects. Section 322 requires that local as well as state governments prepare mitigation plans before they are eligible for both postdisaster mitigation funds (HMGP) and new predisaster funds made available in the 2000 act. Washington State was the first to draft a state plan, in 2004, and all states were required to submit their plans by November 1, 2004; these plans must be renewed every three years. States that fail to submit plans will lose their eligibility for "nonemergency" assistance under the Stafford Act, which would include HMGP funding. Local governments are also required to plan, at the risk of losing some funding if they fail to do so. Budget cuts during the Bush administration, however, have made this program potentially less effective than it might have been.

While the results of section 404/409 mitigation programs have not been as promising as their proponents had hoped, there have been some positive developments. In particular FEMA created a

Mitigation Directorate to manage the HMGP and to promote the idea of mitigation among state and local governments. But mitigation has not become a quantitatively important part of broader natural hazards policy; the amount of money spent on mitigation under section 404 from 1988 to mid-1996 was less than 2 percent of spending on general disaster relief. The details of why mitigation failed to become a serious element of natural hazards policy are too numerous to be recounted here. Godschalk and his colleagues isolate numerous factors: Communities needed to experience a disaster *before* getting HMGP funds, section 409 plans were often pro forma exercises unrelated to actual projects funded under section 404, and the projects funded with HMGP funds bore little or no resemblance to the state 409 plans (Godschalk et al. 1998). While the 2000 act provided for some predisaster mitigation, the amounts available were so small as to be relatively ineffective in promoting efforts that would mitigate moderate or large disasters.

From a learning perspective, it is most interesting that hazard mitigation funding under the Stafford Act is triggered by an actual disaster rather than by attempts to mitigate potential disasters. This policy design contradicts the scientific and technical consensus that mitigation should occur *before* disasters occur so as to reduce the ultimate costs of relief and recovery. Of course, the postdisaster phase would be a good time to try to draw attention to the importance of mitigation, even if experience shows that this is not what happens. Little changed in the Hazard Mitigation and Relocation Assistance Act of 1993, legislation passed in direct response to the flooding of the Midwest in 1993. The 1993 act did amend existing policy by providing a means for property owners in flood-prone areas to sell their property to state governments, which would then mitigate flood hazards. Even with an increase in HMGP money from 10 to 15 percent of federal relief per disaster, however, this act remained a postdisaster program, not the proactive predisaster program for which experts had lobbied.

The Stafford Act's shortcomings in mitigation led to the enactment of the Disaster Mitigation Act of 2000 (DMA, also known as the 2000 Stafford Act Amendments). This act is the first to develop explicitly a predisaster mitigation program for all natural hazards. It created the National Predisaster Mitigation Fund; states and localities are eligible to apply for funds through a proposal process. Such funds may be used to (1) support effective public-private partnerships; (2) improve the assessment of a community's natural hazards vulnerabilities; or (3) establish a community's mitigation priorities. The 2000 act increased the amount of money available under the HMGP from 15 to 20 percent, although budget cuts since then have reduced funding for the program.

These efforts are important because mitigation planning yields tangible benefits (Burby 1994; Burby, French, and Nelson 1998; Dalton and Burby 1994). Indeed, a recent study by the Multi-hazard Mitigation Council of the National Institute of Building Services found that every dollar spent on mitigation yields four dollars in benefits (Multihazard Mitigation Council 2005). But mitigation requires more than federal action. States and local governments must be involved, and success requires broad cooperation among numerous stakeholders. With this in mind, the drafters of the DMA required local governments to develop *local* mitigation plans to complement state mitigation plans (Srinivasan 2003). This is particularly important if localities wish to receive predisaster mitigation funds made available by the DMA. In 2002 FEMA extended the deadline for the preparation of these plans to December 2004. Considerable challenges confront policy-makers who seek to change individual and community behaviors to mitigate disasters. Some political constituencies deny the need for more disaster mitigation efforts (Alesch and Petak 1986; Briechle 1999; Rossi, Wright, and Weber-Burdin 1982), or believe that traditional structural policies, such as the building of levees or other engineered solutions, are as effective as nonstructural mitigation in protecting lives and property.

Many of the activities called for in the DMA were consistent with FEMA's now defunct Project Impact (PI), which was created in 1997 to build public-private partnerships and broad local commitment to hazard mitigation. Few disasters tested the effectiveness of PI, however. The most often cited example of a disaster to strike a PI community was the 2001 Nisqually earthquake that struck near Olympia, Washington, and was felt in the western parts of Washington, British Columbia, and Oregon. The relatively small amount of damage done in Seattle was attributed to the success of PI and its very active and engaged local advocates (see, for example, *Congressional Record,* March 1, 2001, S. 1742). This outcome buttresses findings in 2000 that

> [w]ith respect to communitywide mitigation activities, the data . . .
> indicate that there has been an increase in the types of mitigation
> activities that are being undertaken. Improvement is particularly
> marked among communities that initially had not been as actively
> involved in mitigation projects. Structural and non-structural miti-
> gation programs that are being undertaken include improving land
> use management, removing nonstructural hazards from buildings,
> developing and implementing tool lending programs, elevating
> structures, protecting lifeline facilities, and acquiring flood-
> damaged property (Tierney 2000, 2).

In short, PI seemed to be making headway toward encourag-
ing local action in the mitigation of disasters. This program was
created by FEMA, reaffirmed by the DMA, and yet the Bush administration killed the project in 2001, claiming that it was ineffective. Some members of Congress objected, in some cases
strenuously, but their attempts to restore $25 million to the pro-
gram were defeated. The proponents of PI could point to little
firm evidence of PI's effectiveness because the program was so
new. Evidence that PI was moving in the right direction and was
likely to increase disaster mitigation at the local level was not
enough to save the project. FEMA terminated it rather easily, both
because it was an executive initiative of James Lee Witt rather than
a congressional mandate and because few local champions of PI
rose up with the same passion demonstrated by a very few members of Congress. The project died, and nothing was slated to
replace it by September 11, 2001, after which emergency preparedness and management priorities changed so rapidly that any
arguments for a new PI-type project were overwhelmed by events.
Indeed, the combination of September 11 and FEMA's demotion
to a subunit of the Department of Homeland Security has rendered FEMA's mitigation strategies much less potent than they
were during the Clinton–Witt era.

Returning once again to the normative question, there is considerable evidence in the history of hazards policymaking that the
idea of mitigation has been adopted and written into law. Whether
this increased attention to mitigation has led to long-term changes

in behavior on the part of federal, state, and local officials is unclear. At this point it is safe to say that behavior has not been altered: The political benefits of immediate and plentiful disaster relief are much greater than the benefits of distributing the same amount of money in a more targeted way to mitigate the most pressing hazards.

There is substantial reason to believe that many gains made in natural hazard mitigation—both in terms of increased openness to the idea of mitigation and in actual mitigation policies—have been lost as FEMA and natural hazards programs across agencies have been overshadowed by efforts to address real or perceived "homeland security" threats. Even before September 11, 2001, it was clear that the Bush administration was unlikely to promote the sorts of mitigation measures that had proved during the 1990s to be effective in reducing damage. In 2001 FEMA administrator Joseph Allbaugh, visiting flooded communities in Iowa, upbraided Davenport, Iowa, for failing to build a floodwall to prevent flood damage: "Davenport officials bristled Tuesday at a remark made by Federal Emergency Management Agency Director Joe Allbaugh, who planned to visit the city Thursday to discuss the problem of continual federal bailouts for flood victims. 'The question is: How many times does the American taxpayer have to step in and take care of this flooding, which could be easily prevented by building levees and dikes?' Allbaugh told reporters" (Associated Press 2001). Davenport had chosen not to build a floodwall because of aesthetics and because of local officials' belief that land-use planning would be more effective at mitigating natural disasters.

This incident demonstrates that the Bush administration's attitudes toward hazard mitigation are less sophisticated and informed than those of Bill Clinton and James Lee Witt. Earthquakes and hurricanes are contained within a broader context of natural hazards policy that, since the enactment of the Homeland Security Act in 2003, has become part of an even broader context of homeland security policy. FEMA is a relatively small part of this picture. Earthquakes and hurricanes draw attention to larger questions in natural hazards policy and in emerging notions of "homeland security" as contained in the "all-hazards" approach to natural and humanly caused disasters. Given the new demands placed on local government for homeland security, and given these governments' lack of resources to meet these demands, it is unlikely that the federal government will be able or willing to actively pursue more aggressive mitigation strategies in the future. Indeed, as Hurricane Katrina revealed, the Bush administration actually took steps to make FEMA and its mitigation programs less effective; at the same time, FEMA is less able to respond effectively to natural hazards than it was during the Clinton–Witt years.

Earthquakes and Hurricanes on National and Local Agendas

To assess the extent to which the national government learns from disasters, I considered the influence of these events on the national public agenda as measured by stories in the *New York Times*. Do these news stories discuss substantive policy matters (which are generally rarely covered by the news media), or do they focus on the most obvious objective features of the event—the magnitude of the earthquake, the category or wind speeds of the hurricane—without any particular reference to policy? Do natural disasters trigger coverage of the underlying scientific issues raised by an event—engineering, seismology, or meteorology, for example—which would suggest the possibility for learning to occur?

The results of the analysis of stories in the *New York Times* from January 1990 through October 2002 are shown in table 4.2. The contrasts between hurricanes and earthquakes are striking.

The first and most obvious difference is that coverage of hurricanes is much more event driven than coverage of earthquakes is. Journalists cover hurricanes when one is imminent or has just struck. Typically, there is very little discussion about the science or the risk of a future event. Indeed, there is so little discussion of the potential risk posed by hurricanes that there was no reason to create a category for "stories about potential hurricanes" parallel to similar stories about potential earthquakes. The earthquake domain is full of stories about the possibility of bigger and more damaging earthquakes in the future. Many stories that are not directly about earthquakes—stories about where to site nuclear power plants and other hazardous facilities, for example—address the risk of earthquake. Thus, while 46 percent of the

Table 4.2 Substance of Stories on Earthquakes and Hurricanes in the *New York Times*, 1990–2002 (percent)

Topics	Hurricane			Earthquake		
	Any Event	*No Event*	*Total*	*Any Event*	*No Event*	*Total*
Damage	10	8	10	49	6	23
Future Threats	—	—	—	17	14	15
Mitigation	4	23	5	16	5	9
Objective Size	6	8	6	53	20	33
Preparedness	13	—	13	5	3	4
Recovery	28	—	27	29	2	13
Relief	14	—	14	17	1	7
Response	1	—	1	9	—	4
Science	4	46	6	19	14	16
N	*363*	*13*	*376*	*135*	*210*	*345*

Note: Totals may exceed 100 percent because stories overlap categories.

stories about hurricanes not written about an actual hurricane are about science—primarily about the forecasting of hurricanes—this represents only six stories, as compared to twenty-nine stories about the science of earthquakes when there is no event on the agenda. And when a hurricane is on the agenda, the science of hurricanes—how they form, why they are hazardous, how they are forecast—receives far less attention than the science of earthquakes does in earthquake stories; recent earthquakes actually trigger slightly greater discussion of scientific matters.

New York Times coverage of earthquakes focused more on the damage done than coverage of hurricanes did. This may have something to do with the different features of the two types of disaster: Almost all earthquakes do considerable damage, while a hurricane can pass by without doing much damage or can veer off without causing any damage at all. Proportionally, there are more stories about hurricane preparedness than about earthquake preparedness, because hurricanes can be more accurately forecast, their progress tracked day by day and hour by hour. Earthquakes offer no similar warning, and so there is no buildup of anticipation before an earthquake; the news media thus provide little coverage about earthquake preparedness.

Discussions of objective size are considerably greater in earthquake coverage because journalists have a ready measure of earthquake size, even for small earthquakes that cause little damage: the moment magnitude scale, which has generally replaced the Richter scale.[1] The measurement of the magnitude of earthquake energy is more finely tuned than the Saffir–Simpson hurricane scale, which rates hurricanes from Category 1 (winds at 74 to 95 mph) to Category 5 (winds in excess of 156 mph). Interestingly, the Saffir–Simpson scale was developed with an eye toward creating a measure as useful as the Richter scale, although the scale's focus on damage, not on energy per se, puts it more on a par with the modified Mercalli index, a qualitative scale of earthquake effects ranging from I (not felt; marginal and long period effects of large earthquakes) to XII (damage nearly total; large rock masses displaced; lines of sight and level distorted; objects thrown into the air).[2] Clearly, this qualitative scale does not reflect the actual energy of the earthquake. Because scientists are more likely to quote the moment magnitude scale, the Mercalli index is rarely reported in news stories. In any event, the Saffir–Simpson scale has not been used as often in popular media as the Richter scale and its variants in earthquake-prone areas. This may well have changed, however, with Hurricane Katrina.

Finally, table 4.2 shows that there are important differences in the news coverage of earthquakes and hurricanes regarding mitigation. The large proportion of stories about mitigation in the absence of an actual hurricane is the result of the very small proportion of stories that are not about particular hurricanes. The overall proportion of stories about mitigating the impact of hurricanes is about half that of earthquakes.

Earthquakes and hurricanes, obviously, are local events that damage a relatively small area. A comparison of local news stories to national ones enables us to determine whether local media cover things that national reporters miss, things that therefore may be useful in the policy learning process. I therefore used the Lexis-Nexis database to review local newspaper coverage of two major earthquakes, Northridge (1994) and Nisqually (2001), and two major hurricanes, Andrew (1992) and Floyd (1999). To assess how the local media covered these events, I used LexisNexis to find all articles about the particular hazard in the six months after the disaster and coded the headlines using the same policy categories that I used to code *New York Times* stories. For the earthquakes, I coded headlines in the *San Francisco Chronicle* and the *Seattle Times*; for hurricanes, the *St. Petersburg Times* and the *Raleigh News and Observer*.[3] Coding stories about the same event in papers in two states allowed me to assess whether an event in one state influenced the agenda in another state exposed to a similar hazard. The results are shown in table 4.3.

In the earthquake domain, all the papers paid much greater attention to mitigation compared with the hurricane domain, and the role of science and the risk of future disasters or "aftershocks" were discussed much more frequently. This disparate attention to mitigation and science is also noticeable in interest group activity in congressional hearings, as discussed below.

Group Activity and Congressional Committees

As I argued in chapter 1, a focusing event should mobilize particular kinds of groups to talk about particular kinds of things after a major disaster. Table 4.4 shows the types of groups that appeared before congressional committees to discuss policy matters relating to earthquakes and hurricanes.

There are clearly important differences between the types of people who appear before committees that address earthquakes and those that address hurricanes. In particular, experts who testify about earthquake mitigation are much more prominent when an earthquake is on the agenda than is expert opinion in the hurricane domain. Indeed, hurricane experts are *less* likely to testify before congressional committees when a hurricane is fresh on the agenda; they are twice as likely to testify when no major event is on the agenda.

By contrast, federal officials dominate testimony about hurricanes when a particular event is on the agenda. Local government officials are prominent in both the earthquake and hurricane domains. Indeed, local officials are more prominent in dealing with the earthquake hazard when an event is on the agenda than

Table 4.3 Local Newspaper Coverage of Selected Natural Hazards (percent)

Topics	Earthquakes				Hurricanes		
	San Francisco Chronicle *Northridge*	Seattle Times *Northridge*	San Francisco Chronicle *Nisqually*	Seattle Times *Nisqually*	Raleigh News and Observer *Floyd*	St. Petersburg Times *Floyd*	St. Petersburg Times *Andrew*
Mitigation	15.6	13.5	21.1	20.4	5.1	1.4	5.5
Insurance	9.1	16.2	3.5	1.4	1.4	1.4	3.1
Science/Risk	5.4	2.7	21.1	13.6	0.5	—	—
N	*186*	*37*	*57*	*147*	*434*	*72*	*420*

N = Number of stories in these papers about the event for six months after it occurred.

Table 4.4 Earthquakes and Hurricanes: Congressional Testimony by Group Type and Event Status, 1990–2002 (percent)

Group Type	Earthquake			Hurricane		
	Any Event	*No Event*	*Total*	*Any Event*	*No Event*	*Total*
Attorneys	2.5	0.8	1.2	1.7	0.7	1.1
Citizens and Victims	7.4	—	1.8	1.7	0.7	1.1
Experts	22.2	13.3	15.5	5.1	12.1	9.0
Federal Officials	16.0	43.0	36.4	34.2	16.8	24.4
Foreign Governments	—	—	—	3.4	0.7	1.9
Interest Groups	6.2	16.5	13.9	12.8	22.8	18.4
Local Officials	30.9	4.4	10.9	15.4	5.4	9.8
Other	4.9	2.0	2.7	0.9	2.0	1.5
Private Individuals	—	11.2	8.5	11.1	23.5	18.0
State Officials	9.9	7.2	7.9	12.0	14.8	13.5
Unions	—	1.6	1.2	1.7	0.7	1.1
N	*81*	*249*	*330*	*117*	*149*	*266*

Note: Rounded percentages may not sum to 100 percent.

are local officials in hurricanes. The reasons for this will become clearer when we see how the "local" earthquake policy domain is organized as compared with the national domain. For now we can conclude that expertise—an important part of the learning process—plays a far greater role in earthquakes than in hurricanes, particularly when an event is fresh on the agenda.

The Substance of the Debate

Tables 4.5 and 4.6 show the broader institutional agendas in natural disasters in terms of the substance of testimony provided by witnesses at congressional hearings as reflected in the *Congressional Record*. I used a very conservative coding scheme that coded an event as being about a specific earthquake or hurricane only if the event was mentioned by name, date, or rough geographic area— for example, the Loma Prieta earthquake could also be identified as the San Francisco earthquake. I have included the statements in the *Congressional Record* because they help us gain a sense of the

Table 4.5 Witnesses on Earthquakes and Hurricanes by Agenda Status of Events and by Issue, 1990–2002 (percent)

Issues	Earthquakes			Hurricanes		
	Any Event	No Event	All Testimony	Any Event	No Event	All Testimony
Preparedness	10.8	4.0	5.8	2.7	—	1.4
Response	34.3	12.0	18.0	41.3	10.8	26.6
Recovery and Relief	33.3	20.4	23.8	31.3	11.5	21.8
Mitigation, General	3.9	12.0	10.1	—	7.2	3.5
Mitigation, Nonstructural	3.9	22.5	17.5	3.3	4.3	3.8
Mitigation, Structural	7.8	5.5	6.1	0.7	8.6	4.5
Insurance	5.9	23.6	18.8	20.7	57.6	38.4
N	102	275	378	150	139	289

Note: Rounded percentages may not sum to 100 percent.

Table 4.6 *Congressional Record* **Entries on Earthquakes and Hurricanes by Agenda Status of Events and by Issue, 1990–2002 (percent)**

Entries	Earthquake			Hurricane		
	Any Event	*No Event*	*Total*	*Any Event*	*No Event*	*Total*
Relief/Assistance	37.00	34.70	35.30	24.20	39.80	32.30
Recovery/ Reconstruction	10.90	0.70	3.20	1.10	8.70	5.10
Mitigation	—	6.90	5.30	—	7.80	4.50
Preparedness	—	1.40	1.10	—	1.90	1.00
Response	4.30	6.90	6.30	2.10	6.80	4.50
NEHRA	—	13.90	10.50	—	1.00	0.50
Research	—	0.70	0.50	—	—	—
Insurance	—	2.80	2.10	—	3.90	2.00
N	*46*	*144*	*190*	*95*	*103*	*198*

Note: Rounded percentages may not sum to 100 percent.

attitudes both of "specialist" members of Congress, whose attitudes are more likely to be reflected in the types of witnesses they call to testify, and of the rank-and-file members, whose attitudes are more likely to be reflected in the *Congressional Record.*

The data suggest that neither discussion in the *Congressional Record* nor testimony at hearings has been particularly driven by events. When events do drive testimony or statements, the subjects of discussion are of the sort typical after disasters. Relief and assistance dominate the statements in the *Congressional Record,* in large part because these issues are immediate and pressing in the wake of a disaster. Many of these are statements by local representatives calling for aid in their regions, or by others sympathetic to victims of a particular kind of disaster.

The same pattern appears in congressional testimony, where witnesses' statements are mostly about relief and recovery, with relatively little disaster-driven discussion of mitigation. The *Congressional Record* testimony suggests that rank-and-file members of Congress with no particular interest or expertise in natural hazards policy continue to support the usual sort of postdisaster relief to which the nation has become accustomed since at least the early 1950s. The key differences between earthquakes and hurricanes when no recent events are on the agenda are noteworthy. Mentions of mitigation combined with discussions of the National Earthquake Hazards Reduction Act (NEHRA), a policy specifically designed to aid in the mitigation of earthquake hazards, far exceed the proportion of entries that mention mitigation in the context of hurricanes.

The range of issues Congress considers in hearings is broader than the issues discussed in the *Congressional Record*. Legislative attention is clearly oriented toward disaster relief and assistance, but in the case of earthquakes, mitigation is more than twice as likely to be a subject of legislation than it is in the case of hurricanes. If we include the NEHRA, then legislators pay much greater attention to mitigation of earthquake hazards than to mitigation of hurricane hazards. Surprisingly, the question of insurance comes up twice as often in earthquake legislation as it does in hurricane bills, perhaps because earthquake insurance is much harder to get and is more expensive to purchase than is insurance against the flood and wind risks that accompany hurricanes. Indeed, the difficulty of creating an insurance program for earthquakes may be the reason why so much attention has been paid to other forms of earthquake mitigation. By contrast, flood insurance is a popular, federally subsidized program that aids residents of areas prone to inundation from hurricane rains or storm surges, and this may explain the relatively low level of interest in other forms of hurricane mitigation (table 4.7).

The existence of the NEHRA and NEHRP drives much of the earthquake mitigation discussion; if a similar program were created for hurricanes, we might well see greater discussion of hurricane mitigation (Birkland 1997b). Indeed, the American Association for Wind Engineering and other groups successfully lobbied for passage of the National Windstorm Reduction Act of 2004, a law patterned on the National Earthquake Hazards Reduction Act and contained as part of the NEHRA's reauthorization (in Title II) (HR 2608, PL 108-360). The real effect of this legislation is still unclear, although it is unlikely that the wind program will be as successful as the NEHRP.

Table 4-7 Policy Types in *Congressional Record* and in Proposed Legislation (percent)

Policy Types	Congressional Record		Proposed Legislation		
	Earthquake	Hurricane	Earthquake	Hurricane	All Natural Disasters
Appropriation	15.9	13.8	32.3	54.4	37.2
Authorization	7.6	0.5	—	—	37.2
Insurance	2.4	2.1	28.2	15.0	7.8
Mitigation	5.9	4.6	16.1	7.2	6.2
NEHRA	11.8	0.5	16.9	3.3	1.9
Preparedness	1.2	1.0	—	—	1.6
Recovery/Reconstruction	3.5	5.1	4.8	6.7	5.0
Relief/Assistance	36.5	32.8	25.8	27.2	25.2
Research	0.6	—	4.8	5.0	—
Response	7.1	4.6	—	—	1.6
Sense of the House or Senate	1.2	3.6	2.4	3.9	2.3
Expressions of Sympathy	5.3	3.1	8.1	0.6	—
Stafford Act	—	—	2.4	2.8	2.7
N	172	140	124	180	258

Note: Sums may exceed 100 percent because some items fall into more than one category.

The Windstorm Reduction Act was authorized for only $72.5 million for FY 2006–FY 2008. During the same period $544.5 million was authorized for the NEHRP. The wind program is also a rather diffuse program that will respond to wind hazards posed by hurricanes and by other storms such as strong thunderstorms and tornadoes.

In essence, the scientific, social, and political responses to hurricanes are much more disjointed than are the responses to earthquakes. Earthquake hazard policy is much more likely to include input from scientific and technical experts because of the nature of earthquakes—which continue to attract considerable scientific interest—and because there is relatively little that science can do to promote the already well-known steps that could be taken to mitigate hurricanes. Such measures, which would include significant restrictions on the development of shorelines and surrounding areas, would change the nature of the communities most at risk from significant hurricane damage. This change may not be politically or economically realistic. At their most extreme, the most effective land-use policies would entail a retreat from low-lying coastal areas and barrier islands, a strategy that is very unlikely to be broadly adopted.

The failure of all-hazard mitigation policy to gain much attention in public policy is related to very basic issues in this policy domain. Most public officials acknowledge public support for federal, state, and local disaster relief programs, with relatively little interest in mitigation. There are no active, broad-based public interest groups pressing for government action to prevent damage from disasters. There is considerable resistance on the part of some citizens and local governments to enact costly land-use planning and building code measures to prevent harm from a generally unpredictable hazard (May and Birkland 1994). As a result, there is no obvious constituency for policy entrepreneurs to draw upon to advance disaster prevention and mitigation programs, which accounts for the small number of policy entrepreneurs seeking to keep disaster mitigation and damage prevention issues high on the agenda. In the earthquake domain, some experts provide needed expertise and deliver I-told-you-so's in hearings and other forums. In the hurricane domain, political entrepreneurs are sparser. The "disaster problem" thus languishes near the bottom of national, state, and local priorities until the problem is elevated, not by political activity, a change in indicators, or some political perturbation but by a completely exogenous and largely unpredictable event. Scientific and technical experts can then harness the event to show the need for mitigation policies, but for only as long as that window of opportunity remains open.

There are few if any constituencies in the earthquake or hurricane domains, particularly in the predisaster period, that organize on the basis of potential future harm. The only organized groups are technical and scientific experts who deal with earthquakes. Their expertise is far less important in the hurricane than in the earthquake domain (Birkland 1998), which makes the content of table 4.8 rather remarkable: Attention to hurricane mitigation nearly equals attention to earthquake mitigation, although the former drops considerably when a fresh hurricane is on the agenda. By contrast, mitigation remains an important topic in earthquake policy hearings regardless of whether an earthquake has occurred recently. In sum, disaster policy is the province of technical experts or legislative specialists when the problem is on the back burner. When a particular disaster focuses attention, discussions of policy tend to concentrate on deficiencies in the delivery of relief, relegating federal relief agencies to a defensive, subordinate role immediately after a disaster. Policy discussion in the wake of a disaster ultimately advances policy that deals retrospectively with the insufficiencies of disaster relief policy. Policy made in the absence of a recent disaster tends to deal prospectively with future disasters.

Legislation and Regulation

Legislation related directly to earthquakes and hurricanes is summarized in table 4.8. Hurricane legislation is, as expected, heavily oriented toward relief and assistance for victims. Some evidence suggests that Congress is not providing relief to the exclusion of other policy goals, however. Sixty percent of the hurricane legislation addressed insurance and mitigation broadly (although one can argue that insurance is the primary mitigation tool for hurricanes, since many losses are covered by flood insurance). The

Table 4.8   Substance of Disaster Legislation on Earthquakes and Hurricanes, 1990–2002

Category	Hurricanes	Percentage	Earthquakes	Percentage
Insurance	6	60	4	50
Mitigation	6	60	5	63
NEHRA	3	30	5	63
Preparedness	—	—	—	—
Recovery/ Reconstruction	1	10	1	13
Relief/Assistance	9	90	4	50
Research	—	—	—	—
Response		0	—	—
Stafford Act	2	20	—	—
N	*10*	—	*8*	—

Note: Sums are greater than 100 percent because bills can fall into more than one category.

patterns of attention to mitigation in legislation do not differ greatly between earthquakes and hurricanes.

Legislation in the 1990s emphasized mitigation to a greater extent than it had before passage of the 1988 Stafford Act. Two factors contributed to this increase: the growing influence of the professional community that deals with natural hazards and an increasing sense that federal spending for disaster relief and recovery was expanding out of control. Mitigation is still not the sole or even the primary goal of federal disaster policy, and today the role of mitigation in disaster management is seriously tested by the shift in attention to "homeland security" and the assignment of FEMA to the DHS.

In 1993 Congress amended the Stafford Act to provide for a 15 percent share "of the estimated aggregate amount of grants to be made (less any associated administrative costs) under this Act with respect to the major disaster." In the 2003 omnibus budget reconciliation bill, Congress reduced mitigation funding from 15 percent to 7.5 percent in the face of a presidential request to eliminate the HMGP. The Bush administration argued that the HMGP was not cost effective, a point strongly disputed in a letter drafted by the Oklahoma Floodplain Managers Association, which argued that the "HMGP is extremely effective in reducing the impacts of future natural disasters. Mitigation plays a critical role in the post-disaster recovery/reconstruction period and HMGP offers a reliable source of post-disaster funding."[4] By cutting funding for mitigation, the Bush administration has turned its back on years of actual experience. It is unclear whether the administration's hostility to hazard mitigation is based on ideology, on a belief that the funds are better spent elsewhere, or, in the face of considerable contradictory evidence, on a perception that the program is ineffective. The HMGP has survived, however, and other legislation may elevate mitigation to a greater position of prominence.

It is fruitless to search for policy learning in FEMA regulations related specifically to earthquakes and hurricanes. A search of regulations issued by FEMA in the *Federal Register* reveals virtually no regulatory activity that ties a disaster to improved regulatory policy. Indeed, almost all FEMA regulatory activity consists of issuing notices of a given disaster. When FEMA does issue rules or regulations, the vast majority of them concern routine matters involving the Federal Insurance Administration (FIA)'s flood insurance program. To the extent that policy innovation is likely to come in this domain, it will probably come from outside FEMA, although once this innovation yields results, it is likely to find its way into technical guidance documents issued by FEMA.

Learning from Disasters at the State and Local Levels

An important assumption of this study is that natural hazards are national problems but that local governments are best able to respond and take steps to mitigate them. This is significantly different from the case of aviation security, because the regulation of aviation has long been a federal function under the national government's power to regulate interstate commerce. Federal policy on natural hazards, by contrast, places the federal government in a supporting role, although in practice the states are apt to seek federal assistance even for relatively small "disasters." Still, the states must act to make federal leadership effective. In one obvious example—earthquake policy in California—a state government is a national leader in hazard mitigation measures because it has the longest experience with the hazard. State leadership is less obvious in hurricane policy, where several states are equally at risk from hurricanes.

Let us turn now to the questions of whether and what states learn from earthquakes and hurricanes. I am most concerned with what we might call "direct" learning—evidence that a state has changed its policy on the basis of what it learned from a disaster. It is important to note here that states with similar characteristics have long been assumed to borrow policy ideas from other states (Grossback, Nicholson-Crotty, and Patterson 2004; Rogers 1995). Indeed, one of the often-stated virtues of the American federal system is the so-called "laboratory of democracy": the idea that each state has considerable latitude for policy innovation and that when policy ideas seem to work, other states can adopt them. This diffusion of ideas is the lesson drawing that Richard Rose (1993) describes and can be conceptualized as instrumental learning. The diffusion of ideas and information between states has been assumed to be a function of geographical proximity (neighboring states will learn from each other) or ideological similarity (Grossback, Nicholson-Crotty, and Patterson 2004). I assume that what makes states likely to learn from other states' disaster experience is the similarity of their hazard profiles: Washington will learn from what California does with earthquakes; Florida and North Carolina will learn from each other's experience with hurricanes. A fuller examination of the nature of interstate learning and policy diffusion is beyond the scope of this book, but the following narratives of event-related policy learning are important to this study because they suggest a role for state and federal governments.

Earthquake Policy in California

There are two remarkable features of the history of earthquake policy at the federal and state levels: first, that there *is* a history, and second, that it is reasonably well documented. By contrast, there is little similar history of state and federal efforts aimed at hurricanes.

As documented in Carl-Henry Geschwind's remarkable history of the science and politics of earthquakes in California (2001), scientists have been discussing the problems posed by earthquakes—such things as land use (building near active faults) and building code requirements—since at least the 1906 San Francisco earthquake. Whereas local promoters and civic boosters, primarily in the construction and land development industries, denied the importance of the earthquake hazard and the potential severity of future shocks, the 1925 Santa Barbara earthquake and, to a far greater extent, the 1933 Long Beach earthquake, led to a series of policy changes connected to individual events (table 4.9).

There are two primary reasons for this development. The first is that California was an important part of the progressive movement of the early twentieth century, which promoted substantial political reforms, including direct democracy (through the initiative and referendum) and nonpartisanship, particularly at the local government level. Progressivism is also connected to the early conservation movement and to the belief that government and technical experts working together can address and potentially solve some of the most vexing problems of the day. Indeed, one of the first organizations to be actively concerned with earthquakes in California—the Seismological Society of America—was founded by many of the same people who founded the Sierra Club, and out of the same principles: the efficient use of resources, whether they be natural or built environments.

The second reason is a combination of the technical expertise available in California and the manifest evidence of the earthquake hazard. Between 1900 and 1933 three earthquakes—San Francisco, Santa Barbara, and Long Beach—did considerable damage that simply could not be ignored. Between the late 1930s and mid-1960s many structural engineers—an occupation that, in California at least, owed its origin to earthquake engineering—moved into defense research, focusing on the performance of structures in nuclear blasts, features of which resembled earthquakes.

Interest in earthquakes remained moderate until 1964, when the Alaska earthquake rekindled Californians' interest. The Alaska earthquake also brought the federal government into the picture in a way not seen before. The 1964 earthquake struck when Alaska had been a state for barely five years, and its economic development

**Table 4.9   Key Actions in Earthquake Policy, California
and the United States, 1933–2000**

Year	Law	Triggering Event
1933	Field Act	1933 Long Beach
1933	Riley Act	1933 Long Beach
1964–70	National Academy Studies of the Alaska Earthquake	1964 Alaska
1972	Bridge Seismic Retrofit Program	1971 San Fernando
1972	Strong Motion Instrumentation Program	1971 San Fernando
1972	Alquist–Priolo Earthquake Fault Zoning Act	1971 San Fernando
1973	Hospital Safety Act	1971 San Fernando
1975	Seismic Safety Commission Act	1971 San Fernando
1977	National Earthquake Hazards Reduction Act	Various, including 1964 Alaska, 1975 China
1986	California Earthquake Hazards Reduction Act	1985 Mexico City
1986	Unreinforced Masonry Building Law	1983 Coalinga
1986	Essential Services Building Seismic Safety Act	1985 Mexico City
1990	Earthquake Safety and Public Buildings Rehabilitation Bond Act of 1990 (Prop. 122)	1989 Loma Prieta
1990	Seismic Hazards Mapping Act	1989 Loma Prieta
1994	Hospital Seismic Retrofit and Replacement Program	1994 Northridge
1994	Marine Oil Terminal Program	1994 Northridge

Source: California Governor's Office of Emergency Management (2004), 114–18.

was still in its infancy. Alaska relied heavily on traditional industries—timber and fisheries—and on federal aid and spending.
Alaska's infancy as a state attracted federal attention that might not
have been shown other states. Thus President Johnson appointed
the Federal Reconstruction and Development Planning Commission to guide Alaska's recovery from the earthquake and more

broadly its development as a state. The National Research Council also undertook a massive study of the Alaska earthquake that produced a multivolume report on its scientific, engineering, economic, and social impacts. This earthquake was thus among the most studied natural disasters in U.S. history. It rekindled interest in earthquake engineering nationally and in California, and began a process in the federal government that eventually led to the enactment of the National Earthquake Hazards Reduction Act.

The Alaska earthquake did considerable damage to settled areas in south-central Alaska, and Californians could not help but consider the implications of a similar—or even smaller—earthquake for the much more densely populated urban areas of their own state. This became more than speculation at 6:01 AM local time on February 9, 1971, when a magnitude 6.6 earthquake struck the San Fernando Valley area of Los Angeles. This was at least the equal of the 1933 Long Beach temblor as a trigger for policy change in California. This earthquake was not the much-feared "big one," but it did enough damage to raise serious concerns about the prospect of even larger earthquakes in the future.

The 1971 earthquake focused attention on two types of structures that were most dramatically damaged: hospitals and freeway overpasses. The damage to hospitals was particularly troubling, and this earthquake led to the passage of the Alquist–Priolo Act, the Hospital Safety Act, and the Seismic Safety Commission Act. The state's Department of Transportation (CalTrans) embarked on a program to improve the construction and performance of highway overpasses. Indeed, most post-1971 overpasses performed much better in the 1994 Northridge earthquake than did structures built before the 1971 event.

It is difficult, however, to say that any one event by itself yields policy change. John Kingdon notes that any focusing event will yield policy change only if the political environment is receptive to change for other reasons as well, notably the presence of key policy entrepreneurs. Olson (2003) and Geschwind (2001) describe in detail the key policy entrepreneurs—civic leaders, engineers, and earth scientists—who were available to induce state and national legislators to take the earthquake hazard seriously.

After the 1971 earthquake, several events and features of the policy domain came together to make possible the eventual passage of the National Earthquake Hazards Reduction Act in 1977. By 1970 the National Academy of Sciences study of the Alaska earthquake was complete. Then the 1971 San Fernando event triggered an intensive round of research and legislation. In 1976 a magnitude 7.3 earthquake struck Tangshan, in northeastern China, killing more than six hundred thousand people and injuring another seven hundred thousand. This was viewed as particularly tragic in light of what was believed to be the apparently successful prediction of an earthquake in China in 1975, which caused the evacuation of Heicheng, sparing thousands of lives. This prediction, coupled with an increase in what appeared to be precursors of an earthquake along the so-called "Palmdale bulge" in central California, led to a belief among scientists and policymakers that earth scientists were on the verge of being able to predict earthquakes.

The combination of these events, coupled with the actions of policy entrepreneurs such as Senator Alan Cranston (D-CA) and seismologist Frank Press, later the head of the National Academy of Sciences and President Carter's science advisor, led to conditions favorable to the creation of the NEHRA. While the original NEHRA of 1977 focused considerable attention on earthquake prediction, early claims of the short-term usefulness of earthquake prediction were found to be overstated, as later research in the Palmdale Bulge demonstrated. In addition, earth and social scientists became concerned about the social aspects of earthquake predictions, which were likely to be wrong in some cases and to fail to predict actual earthquakes in others. In addition, the economic and social costs of evacuating an area that might be struck by an earthquake were much more profound than had originally been postulated (see, for example, Cochrane et al. 1974; Weisbecker et al. 1977). Prediction later became a much less important aspect of the NEHRA as the focus shifted to mitigating the hazard. Indeed, as Weisbecker and his colleagues found, long-term earthquake predictions should yield the sorts of actions that people should be taking anyway in "earthquake country," but they will not produce significant changes in behavior.

The NEHRP led to considerable research on earthquakes and related natural hazards and played an important role in researching mitigation measures and putting them into practice. The program encouraged intensive research on the effects of the 1989

Loma Prieta and 1994 Northridge earthquakes. These quakes led to policy changes in California, though not as dramatic as the ones that followed the 1971 San Fernando quake. Many of the post-1989 changes sought to consolidate the gains in legislation passed after 1971, such as the 1990 bond act that funded the retrofitting shown to be needed after the 1971 and 1989 earthquakes.

We can say with confidence that not every damaging earthquake in California has led to substantial policy change, but that the largest earthquakes there since 1933 have been clearly linked to some sort of policy change in the immediate aftermath of these events. Such changes are examples of instrumental learning; as events happen, policymakers learn better ways to mitigate their hazards. We can see substantial evidence of social policy learning and political learning as well. Social policy learning in California involved learning about how the earthquake hazard is constructed and understood. In the early 1900s the earthquake hazard was seen as being minor and localized, and comparisons were made between the small toll of earthquakes and the much larger toll of other natural hazards in other parts of the nation. By 1933, however, the substantial damage done to schools provided proponents of improved buildings a powerful image that boosters, builders, and real estate interests could not ignore. The professional community was able to use the Long Beach earthquake to make the economic and political argument that it was in building owners' own economic interest to construct buildings in ways that might reduce damage and minimize their potential economic losses.

Earthquake Policy in Washington State

The popular perception is that earthquakes are largely a California phenomenon, and that of all the states most at risk for a catastrophic earthquake, California is at the top of the list. And it is true that California tops FEMA's list of the thirty-nine states at risk for earthquakes. But Washington, according to FEMA, is the number-two state in terms of its exposure to potentially catastrophic earthquake damage.

I chose Washington State for comparison with California because the most intensively developed area of the state is at risk for a catastrophic earthquake. This area extends over about one hundred miles, from Everett in the north to Olympia in the south, and is home to more than 3.4 million people. As stated in the Washington State Hazard Mitigation Plan:

> Evidence points to a magnitude 7 or greater earthquake on the Seattle fault about 900 A.D. Such evidence includes a tsunami, deposit in Puget Sound, landslides in Lake Washington, rockslides on nearby, mountains, and a seven-meter uplift of a marine terrace.
>
> An earthquake with such a magnitude today would cause tremendous damage and economic disruption throughout the central Puget Sound region. Preliminary estimates of damage and loss developed for a multi-disciplinary group preparing a scenario for a magnitude 6.7 event on the fault showed such a quake would result in extensive or complete damage to more than 58,000 buildings with a loss of $36 billion, more than 55,000 displaced households, and up to 2,400 deaths and 800 injuries requiring hospitalization. (Washington 2004, Tab 7.1.3, p. 5)

While Washington's mitigation plan notes that there have been several earthquakes in eastern Washington, in the past seventy-five years there have been only three earthquakes of magnitude 6.0 or greater, and all of these were in the Puget Sound region. Indeed, the epicenters of these three earthquakes were within about forty-five miles of each other (table 4.10).

Nearly all of the populated area of the Puget Sound basin falls within the zone in which there is a 10 percent probability of ground motion of 30 percent of the force of gravity (.3g) in the next fifty years (Washington 2004, Tab 7.1.3, p. 2). One might therefore expect to see significant efforts in the state to address the earthquake threat, including mitigation strategies. FEMA lists Seattle seventh on a list of annualized earthquake losses for all U.S. cities; Tacoma is twenty-second.

Despite these facts, Washington state law is much less extensive in its discussion of earthquake hazard mitigation than is California law. Washington's hazard mitigation plan identifies only three primary legislative enactments that indirectly serve to mitigate earthquakes. In 1955 the legislature established a minimum level of building performance for "hospitals, schools, except one story, portable, frame school buildings, buildings designed or constructed as places of assembly accommodating more than three

Table 4.10   Earthquakes of Magnitude 6.0 or Greater, Washington State since 1900

Date	Depth	Moment Magnitude	Location
April 13, 1949	54.0 km	7.1	12.3 km ENE of Olympia
April 29, 1965	57.0 km	6.5	18.3 km N of Tacoma
February 28, 2001	51.9 km	6.8	17.0 km NE of Olympia

Source: State of Washington Military Department, Emergency Management Division (2004).

hundred persons; and all structures owned by the state, county, special districts, or any municipal corporation within the state of Washington" (Revised Code of Washington [RCW] 70.86.020). This law is out of date, having been substantially superseded by improved building code provisions. The second legal requirement is contained in the Growth Management Act of 1990 (RCW 36.70A), which requires that cities and counties "identify and protect critical areas such as frequently flooded areas and geologically hazardous areas, and for the fastest-growing counties (and their cities) to develop comprehensive land use plans to limit growth to identified urban growth areas." The law also allows, but does not require, communities to prepare natural hazard elements of their local comprehensive plans. The state provides technical support for such efforts. Finally, the state of Washington has adopted in the state building code (RCW 19-27 and Washington Administrative Code title 51) the provisions of the International Building Code (IBC), the successor to the Uniform Building Code (UBC). California's structural engineers were among the leaders in the development of the UBC, and many seismic provisions have been added and improved upon for the new IBC.

Washington's earthquake program in the Emergency Management Division of the Military Department also works to mitigate earthquakes. This program, funded under NERHP, is "designed to enhance seismic safety in support of the state's role in implementing the National Earthquake Hazards Reduction Program." The program's website is cursory and nowhere near as comprehensive in its consideration of the earthquake hazard as that of the California Seismic Safety Commission.[5]

We can conclude from the legislative and administrative record that Washington State has taken important steps to reduce its vulnerability to earthquakes. It is not my intention to suggest that Washington's efforts to mitigate earthquake hazards fall short of what is suggested by the risk profile of the region. My interest here is in whether we can attribute legislative and other policy change to some sort of learning process linked to particular disasters. While such changes were largely driven by earthquake experience in California, they are less clearly linked to specific events in Washington's seismic history. Instead, they are more clearly a function of some degree of earthquake experience, particularly in California, which drives federal efforts to pressure earthquake-prone states, including Washington, to be more attentive to the earthquake hazard. To the extent that Washington's building codes have changed to reflect the state's experience with earthquakes, this is the result of a broad review of the building codes rather than the experience of a particular earthquake. This is also true in California, but municipalities in California have shown greater willingness to amend local building codes to address problem structures such as unreinforced masonry buildings.

From this evidence we can conclude that Washington has not learned from the accumulation of earthquake experience the way California has. The state has not enacted laws that would mitigate earthquake damage to schools, hospitals, highways, and unreinforced masonry buildings to the same extent that California has. Moreover, there is little evidence that the occurrence of earthquakes has given proponents of mitigation better arguments; had such arguments been made, it is likely that policy would have changed in the ways it has in California. California's leadership role is crucial in the earthquake policy domain.

Hurricane Policy in Florida and North Carolina

Hurricane policy has less history than earthquake policy because federal involvement is much less direct and pronounced. The relative lack of federal involvement in hurricane mitigation is the result of lower levels of group mobilization in the hurricane domain.

Moreover, the mobilization that has occurred has probably had a greater influence at the state than at the local level. A review of the history of policymaking relating to hurricanes in Florida and North Carolina is instructive. Hurricanes were watershed events in these states and they induced policy changes that appear to reflect policy learning within both states.

Florida

Although Florida is more prone to hurricanes than any other state, the most populated areas of Florida—particularly the southern areas of Miami and Tampa Bay—had not experienced many severe hurricanes until Hurricane Andrew struck in 1992. Hurricane Andrew was a Category 4 storm, the eye of which passed about twenty miles south of Miami; had the storm come ashore further north, the damage and loss of life might have been much greater.

Of course, Florida was well aware of its hurricane hazard before Hurricane Andrew struck. Three of the five most damaging hurricanes to hit the United States from 1900 to 1997 struck Florida. As a result, the governor and legislature have taken steps to be better prepared for hurricanes and to mitigate their damage. Preparedness, response (including evacuation), and recovery appear to have played a prominent role in their deliberations.

Elliott Mittler notes that efforts to coordinate disaster management in Florida began in 1981, when the Florida Department of Community Affairs (DCA) sought to integrate physical and social features of disaster planning and management into "Comprehensive Emergency Management" or CEM. "The final recommendation of the DCA was a proposed state hazard mitigation program to be managed by Bureau of Disaster Preparedness (now the Division of Emergency Management) within DCA. It contained three elements, (1) hurricane evacuation planning, (2) the development and maintenance of the Florida Comprehensive Emergency Management Plan, and (3) the development of administrative rules to define procedures which must be followed by local governments to produce uniformly developed local and state emergency management plans and a state plan review process" (Mittler 1998). These three elements clearly did not emphasize mitigation as it is commonly understood, but they did acknowledge that preparedness was important to reducing losses.

Just as the federal government formed commissions to study aviation security, Florida established several study commissions to examine hurricane policies and make recommendations. A key difference is that some of these commissions were created not in response to an actual disaster but in the awareness of the possibility of disaster.

The first effort in this direction was the Governor's Hurricane Conference, which was first held in 1987 and has now become an annual event. The first conference was held after the evacuation of coastal areas in anticipation of Hurricane Elena, at the request of the Florida Emergency Preparedness Association, a group of local emergency managers. This conference continues to promote knowledge sharing, and it is an opportunity for state managers and FEMA officials to exchange ideas on preparedness. The conference has become an important learning mechanism; its 2005 agenda included several workshops on mitigation, among them "Building Disaster Resistant Communities," "Promoting Successful Mitigation," and "Mitigation Programs."

The Florida legislature has more power than most other state legislatures, and it often initiates action rather than merely react to directions from the governor, who is constitutionally weaker than most governors. Thus in 1989 (before Hurricane Hugo, which did not trigger this action), the speaker of the Florida House created the Speaker's Task Force on Emergency Preparedness. This task force focused more on preparedness and response than on mitigation and it consisted of four subcommittees: (1) Evacuation and Sheltering, (2) Communications, Operations, and Coordination, (3) Funding, and (4) Public Awareness and Education. It is not entirely surprising that mitigation would receive relatively little attention, because it had not yet become an important part of FEMA's efforts in the states; FEMA's Mitigation Directorate was not established until 1994. The task force's key recommendations were oriented primarily toward response and recovery, although they did include one important mitigation measure—a change to building codes "to require hurricane shutters on multi-unit housing."

Legislation was introduced in 1990, 1991, and 1992 that would have restructured emergency management in Florida, but it was not enacted. In 1990 the chair of the "Committee on Emergency Preparedness, Military and Veterans Affairs introduced House Bill

No. 3669 to overhaul the emergency management system in Florida" (Mittler 1998). This bill was intended to enact the recommendations of the speaker's task force. They included, most controversially, an assessment of $2 per policy on homeowners' insurance ($4 per commercial policy) that would have been deposited into a fund to improve response, provide relief for disasters not declared as such by the federal government, provide funds to match federal grants, and defray state emergency management costs. This bill passed in the House but failed in the Senate because senators from northern Florida balked at creating a trust fund that they thought would primarily benefit southern Florida. Similar bills died in 1991 and 1992.

These ideas were resurrected dramatically after Hurricane Andrew. Andrew is widely understood to be the event that forced substantial reform of FEMA; indeed, Andrew almost caused FEMA to be disbanded given its inept response to the storm and its failure to coordinate effectively with Florida officials. Nor did Florida respond well to the emergency. As Mittler puts it:

> What became evident in the first weeks after Andrew was that the FEMA and the overall federal response as well as the Florida response were uncoordinated, confused, and often inadequate. Consequently, in a desire to discover why and to make recommendations for improvement, the Congress requested the National Academy of Public Administration to evaluate the federal emergency management system and FEMA. FEMA requested its Inspector General to conduct a post-disaster audit, and Governor Chiles issued an executive order (92-242) establishing the Governor's Disaster Planning and Response Review Committee "to evaluate current state and local statutes, plans and programs for natural and man-made disasters, and to make recommendations to the Governor and the State Legislature" not later than January 15, 1993. The national emergency management system was acknowledged as being broken, and both the federal government and the state wanted to know why and what should be done to improve it. (Mittler 1997, internal citations omitted)

Federal and state officials realized that Andrew was not the "big storm" that everyone had feared. It was a Category 4 hurricane that passed south of Miami, not the much-feared Category 5 aimed directly at the city. Officials also realized that if response to Andrew was so poor, response to a larger storm in a populated area would probably only be poorer. The Governor's Disaster Planning and Response Review Committee report explicitly acknowledged that it was formed "to ensure Florida *takes advantage of the lessons that can be learned* from Hurricane Andrew to improve emergency preparedness and recovery programs" (Governor's Disaster Planning and Response Review Committee 1993, 1). This document is a key element in the history of hurricane policy in Florida because it encapsulates much of what had already been said about emergency management there. The committee, known as the Lewis Committee after its chair, former state Senate president Philip D. Lewis, made ninety-four specific recommendations. They were intended to improve communications at and among all levels of government, to strengthen plans for evacuation, shelter, and postdisaster response and recovery, to enhance intergovernmental coordination, and to improve training (Governor's Disaster Planning and Response Review Committee 1993, 3).

The Florida legislature took up the recommendations contained in the Lewis Committee report, and once again the House readily passed legislation that implemented many of them, including the $2/$4 surcharge on residential and commercial insurance policies. Some northern and central Florida senators again balked at the surcharge until "several counties in the central and northern parts of the state were hit by a fierce winter storm on March 13 which convinced Senators in those areas that hurricane threats and emergency management were not just south Florida concerns" (Mittler 1997).

Why did the legislation succeed in 1993 when it had failed in 1990 and 1991? Mittler gives several reasons: (1) the recognition that the emergency management system was inadequate to serve the needs of the state in the event of major natural and other disasters; (2) the support of the governor, many legislators, and the emergency management professionals in the state for comprehensive change and a dedicated source of funding; (3) the long-term development of a program of change that had fostered previous legislation, thereby establishing a foundation for the drafting of a new bill; (4) the use of a funding mechanism that did not increase taxes or divert general revenue funds from other programs;

and (5) the winter storm of 1993 in the northern and central part of the state, which convinced senators who had previously opposed the legislation that improved emergency management was a state-wide issue (Mittler 1997).

Mittler argues that the Lewis Committee's recommendations were adopted en masse because of the Florida legislature's rules and short legislative session, which prevents substantial amendments to legislation. But the key catalyst, of course, was Hurricane Andrew, reinforced by the 1993 winter storm, which opened a window of opportunity for the passage of these recommendations.

The Lewis Committee focused primarily on preparedness and coordination. Under the leadership of the Florida DCA, through the Emergency Management, Preparedness, and Assistance Trust Fund, into which policy surcharge funds were deposited, the vast majority of the Lewis Committee's recommendations were implemented. In 1995 the DCA recommended that the state should shift priorities to "refocus on mitigation . . . to reduce [Florida's] vulnerability to loss of life and property" (Florida Department of Community Affairs 1995, 3).

Florida's efforts to mitigate natural hazards are broadly accomplished through two major programs: the comprehensive planning process and the Florida building code. Florida is one of ten states that require at least some communities to prepare comprehensive plans with a natural disaster element, and one of seven that require all communities do so (North Carolina and South Carolina require such planning only in coastal counties, whereas Arizona requires it only in larger cities). California also requires a hazard element in its community plans (Burby 2005). Such a requirement is important: The lack of a state mandate to plan for natural hazards often means that local governments fail to plan for them even when the state requires plans, if it does not explicitly specify a hazard element (May 1993; Steinberg and Burby 2002).

Florida's mandate is quite strong. In a chart titled "State Laws Requiring Attention to Natural Hazards in Comprehensive Plans," Burby describes Florida's planning mandate (in Fla. Stat. 163.3177) as "stringent . . . including state review of plans for consistency with state plan" (Burby 2005, 70). Indeed, Florida was well prepared to meet the requirements of the Disaster Mitigation Act of 2000, which requires local as well as state governments to have mitigation plans in place before they receive HMGP funding. The Florida statute provides for two key elements of local comprehensive plans: "7. Limitation of public expenditures that subsidize development in high-hazard coastal areas. 8. Protection of human life against the effects of natural disasters."

The second program for mitigating hurricane damage is the Florida building code. The history of this building code encompasses years of experience with the damage done by hurricanes and the failure to enforce building codes. Florida's building code was for years considered the most stringent in the nation with respect to hurricane hazards; in particular, special provisions for south Florida (contained in the south Florida building code) made the most hurricane-prone areas of the state subject to the most stringent hurricane building codes in the nation.

Hurricane Andrew put the supposed superiority of building code provisions *and* enforcement in south Florida to the test. Poor enforcement of existing building codes was met with some surprise by many commentators, many of whom noted that the existing codes were among the most stringent in the nation. Andrew revealed that a building code is only as strong as its enforcement (Baker 1993). Many interests argued that such stringent codes carried requirements that were unnecessary in some parts of the state, thereby increasing building costs. One state senator (who is also an architect) from the Florida Panhandle region argued that stringent wind hazard provisions in the building code need not apply to the Panhandle because it is less prone to the most powerful hurricanes. The senator was speaking for opponents of more stringent codes from the construction industry, particularly home builders, whose interests lay in promoting the least stringent codes or in using the least expensive construction methods.[6] Even after Hurricane Andrew builders questioned the need for more stringent codes, particularly in the Panhandle. The insurance industry, on the other hand, cited the huge amounts of damage done by wind and advocated more stringent codes. According to the ISO (formerly known as the Insurance Service Office), the majority of the insurance industry's catastrophic losses since 1986 have been from windstorms (ISO Properties 2005).

Ultimately a compromise was reached: New provisions were added to the Florida building code that incorporated much of the SFBC's provisions for wind resistance. Buildings were to be made less prone to damage from wind-driven projectiles; protection could be gained through special damage-resistant glass or through storm shutters. Insurance companies were to provide cost reductions on premiums for buildings so equipped; this reduced insurance cost was one of the reasons for the adoption of the changes. However, the Panhandle was excluded from the new requirement in the mistaken belief that risks in the western part of the state were not as high as in south Florida. Homes built in the Panhandle region needed only to withstand 120-mile-per-hour winds within one mile of the beach, a much less stringent standard than the code applied to the rest of the state. Hurricane Ivan, one of three storms that struck Florida in 2004, led to some discussion of improving wind-hazard standards in the Panhandle. On May 10, 2005, a "hurricane research advisory committee," appointed by the chair of the Florida Building Commission to investigate building failures after the 2004 hurricane season, recommended among other things that the so-called Panhandle exemption be eliminated with respect to resistance to windborne debris. The 2004 hurricane season, and the damage done by Hurricane Katrina along the Gulf Coast in 2005, may have tilted the balance in favor of the more stringent building code in the Panhandle, but this matter is hardly settled. Legislation to implement such a change may be introduced in the 2006 legislative session, but in the meantime the legislature avoided the issue in 2005 by asking the state Building Commission for a study to determine whether the more stringent code would reduce damage. The construction lobby in particular continues to argue that there is little difference between damage to buildings built to 2002 building code standards and damage to those that did not comply with the standards (Dunkelberger 2005). In sum, we can say that Hurricane Ivan led to a learning process in that legislators and others seemed open to considering new information gleaned from the 2004 hurricane season. We cannot, however, find evidence of actual instrumental learning because the policy instrument—the building code—has not demonstrably changed. But the matter is not yet settled.

Have the changes since Hurricane Andrew been put to the test? While no storm as severe as Andrew has struck the state since, it is generally believed that state and federal officials were well prepared for Hurricane Ivan, that they responded well, and that structures built to more stringent code requirements did fare well in the storms that did strike. Indeed, the successful federal response to the 2004 hurricane season may have lulled FEMA into a belief that it could effectively handle Hurricane Katrina, which it manifestly did not do. Ivan demonstrated that no part of Florida was immune to hurricanes. While one might quibble over the failure of the Florida building code to be applied to the Panhandle, the land-use planning and high-velocity wind requirements in the one-mile zone probably did reduce damage and injuries.

In the end, Hurricane Andrew accomplished two things. It revealed shortcomings in the enforcement of building codes, and it revealed problems with interagency coordination, preparedness, and response. It appears that responses to the 2004 storms were much improved over the response to Hurricane Andrew. It seems unlikely that improved emergency management and mitigation strategies would have been adopted in the absence of this hurricane. Andrew led to instrumental policy learning about the substance and enforcement of building codes. It also led to some political learning in that it provided proponents of mitigation with good object lessons in hurricane mitigation, which they used to promote better hurricane mitigation. And there was some clear social policy learning: Hurricane Andrew taught residents that hurricanes were not freak storms or random acts of nature; Floridians learned that human institutions and decisions had a real influence on whether a community suffered substantial hurricane damage.

North Carolina

The historical record suggests that North Carolina's hurricane mitigation is much less a function of changes that follow a specific disaster than is the case in Florida. It seems to be more the product of an accumulation of disaster experience, both in North Carolina and other states, and a reasonably strong commitment to land-use planning and hazard mitigation strategies, particularly along the coast.

Three key milestones have been reached in North Carolina. The first was the establishment of FEMA's Mitigation Directorate, which led some states to emulate FEMA's efforts. North Carolina was an early and relatively enthusiastic student of mitigation principles and techniques, but it took a catalytic event before the state actually adopted them. That event was Hurricane Fran in 1996 (the second milestone), a Category 3 storm that did at least $4 billion in damage (Whitlock and Williams 1996). This disaster illustrates how even moderately large storms can do substantial damage as coastal areas grow much faster than inland areas, exposing far more people and property to wind, flooding, and storm surges. Fran led Governor Jim Hunt, in October 1996, to create the North Carolina Disaster Recovery Task Force, which in the remarkably short span of 127 days issued eighty-four recommendations drafted by seven subcommittees (or "action teams," in the task force's parlance). Not long afterward the North Carolina Division of Emergency Management noted that "38 [of the recommendations] are completed, 44 are progressing, and 2 are delayed."[7]

Perhaps the most important policy outcome from a mitigation perspective was the creation of the Hazard Mitigation Section of the North Carolina Department of Emergency Management. As the draft state mitigation plan notes:

The Hazard Mitigation Section . . . was primarily tasked with channeling 110 million dollars through the federal Hazard Mitigation Grant Program (HMGP). These funds have been used to carry out a variety of mitigation initiatives: elevation-in-place of flood-prone structures, acquisition of damaged or hazard-prone structures; public education and warning projects; and support for the development of the State's local Hazard Mitigation Planning Initiative (HMPI).

In essence, when Hurricane Floyd struck in September 1999— three years following Fran—the Mitigation Section was already on its way to institutionalizing a "mitigation ethic" in communities across the state. New groups and organizations in the public, private, voluntary, and research sectors were becoming directly involved in projects and initiatives to reduce the vulnerability of North Carolina communities to hurricanes and other natural hazards. During the aftermath of Floyd, the Mitigation Section has been able to capitalize by gaining even more support for mitigation, engaging even more partners, and broadening the application of mitigation practices to meet multiple objectives that go beyond solely reducing hazard vulnerability. (North Carolina Division of Emergency Management 2004, part II, 11–12)

This account of North Carolina's embrace of hazard mitigation is consistent with most literature on state-level planning. This commitment to mitigation has been considerably strengthened by legislation enacted in June 2001, popularly called Senate Bill 300. This bill amended North Carolina's emergency management law to parallel federal law closely; it created a new section, NCGS 166A-6A, under subsections (b) (1) (3), that required local communities to adopt hazard mitigation plans before they could receive state aid, and (b) (1) (4), which requires communities to participate in the National Flood Insurance Program (NFIP) in order to receive state flood aid. "The bill represents one of the most significant attempts by a state anywhere in the country to take on a greater role in disaster recovery and mitigation. Senate Bill 300 codified several policy recommendations made by the Disaster Response and Recovery Commission" (University of North Carolina, Office of the President 2001, 33).

Senate Bill 300 goes far beyond the sort of mitigation planning that was likely to occur incidental to, but not directly as a goal of, other state environmental and land-use policies. In particular, the Costal Area Management Act of 1974, as amended, requires each of twenty coastal counties to prepare land-use plans that are consistent with planning goals established by the state of North Carolina.

The third milestone reached in the interim between Hurricane Fran and the passage of Senate Bill 300 was Hurricane Floyd, a Category 2 storm that became North Carolina's costliest natural disaster to date. In contrast with Hurricanes Andrew and Fran, however, the damage done by Floyd was done predominantly by flooding. Rainfall amounted to as much as fifteen to twenty inches in some places. Rivers, most notably the Tar and Neuse, flooded. Entire communities were inundated and damage reached billions of dollars. One of the most profound outcomes of this flooding was the contamination of inland and estuarine waters when many waste lagoons at large-scale hog farms broke or were overtopped by floodwaters. Much of this wastewater ended up in rivers and their estuaries, and in Pamlico Sound, raising considerable fear of massive fish kills and other negative environmental effects. While Floyd most dramatically exemplified the problem of hog waste entering the waters of North Carolina, other storms—Hurricanes Fran in 1996 and Dennis in 1999, for example—also led either to the failure or overtopping of waste lagoons or the washing of hog waste from fields into streams and ultimately into estuaries.

One cannot therefore say that Floyd was the sole event in which this problem arose, but it was the event that ultimately triggered action, for two related reasons. First, the sheer number of hog farms involved—at least forty-six waste lagoons or pits were breached—plus the growing number of such farms in floodplains, led to considerable concern among local residents and environmental officials. Second, dramatic news photos of hogs standing on barn roofs and hog carcasses floating in floodwaters demonstrated the problem to a broad audience and prompted the popular press to run articles citing scientific and lay concerns about the effects of such flooding. As Dr. Steven B. Wing, associate professor of epidemiology at the UNC School of Public Health, noted, "North Carolina's industrial animal operations are currently permitted as non-discharge facilities under the assumption that all waste is contained on site. Our analyses emphasize that this is not the case. Flood conditions occur periodically in the state. As long as there are industrial livestock operations in flood plains, flooding will lead to environmental contamination from chemicals and disease-causing organisms" (Swichtenberg 2002, 8).

It was originally feared that flooding from Floyd would lead to high levels of nutrients running into rivers, estuaries, and the large Pamlico and Albemarle sounds (Harte 2001). Observers expected the environmental impact to be particularly grievous because water remains in the sound for about one year, which meant that the increased nutrient load and decreased salinity could lead, as Paerl and others found, to "a cascading set of physical, chemical, and ecological impacts . . . including strong vertical stratification, bottom water hypoxia, a sustained increase in algal biomass, displacement of many marine organisms, and a rise in fish disease" (Paerl et al. 2001, 5655). Fish kills, however, were much greater during Hurricane Fran in 1996 because of "severe dissolved oxygen deficits and high contaminant loadings (total nitrogen, total phosphorus, suspended solids, and fecal bacteria." Higher water volumes from the 1999 hurricanes (Dennis, Floyd, Irene) "delivered generally comparable but more dilute contaminant loads, and no major fish kills were reported. There were no discernible long-term adverse impacts on water quality," and water quality and biota recovered fairly rapidly (Burkholder et al. 2004, 9291).

The images of so many breached hog ponds (and the accompanying news coverage), combined with the potential for harm to human health from contaminated water supplies, led to action to reduce this threat, primarily in the form of a buyout of existing hog farms in the hundred-year floodplain. Indeed, North Carolina is among the nation's leaders in using hazard mitigation funds to purchase flood-prone properties and remove property from harm's way, allowing the floodplain to work naturally (Regulatory Intelligence Data 1999). One research organization argued that such buyouts would be more likely if North Carolina developed an emergency management trust fund to pay for hazard mitigation (North Carolina Center for Public Policy Research 2001). By late 2001 only fourteen of fifty hog farms in the hundred-year floodplain had been bought out.

Remarkably, Hurricane Floyd did not lead to what may have been the most obvious policy outcome of this storm: more stringent construction standards in floodplains, for both agricultural and residential construction. Ultimately the legislature rejected a requirement that the lowest dwelling floor of a house be built to two feet above the water level expected in a hundred-year (that is, a 1 percent probability) flood. The less stringent NFIP standard of one foot was retained. That said, the existence of a particular elevation standard may be less important than individual property owners' experiences with flooding and their perceptions of the steps necessary to protect their property (Work, Rodgers, and Osborne 1999). When residents have direct experience with flooding, whether from hurricanes or from lesser storms, they are more likely to take whatever mitigation steps they deem necessary, including building the structure to a higher level than required by local or state law.

In North Carolina there is evidence of instrumental policy learning, but such learning is more a product of the accumulation of experience in North Carolina and other states than the result of one individual event. This is not to say that events do not matter in North Carolina but that no single event dominates the policy history of the state the way Hurricane Andrew dominates Florida's hurricane history. Florida also shows considerable evidence of instrumental policy learning, but much of this is associated with one event, Hurricane Andrew. Andrew also enhanced social policy learning by helping people understand the cause of Andrew's widespread damage: the lax enforcement of building codes and the general low level of preparedness. The resulting damage gave proponents of policy change considerable ammunition for arguing in favor of substantive policy change.

Summarizing State-Level Learning

The state-level case studies reveal much about the differences between earthquakes and hurricanes and allow us to better understand learning processes about these disasters at the federal level. In particular, we can make a strong claim that mitigation is more important to participants in earthquakes than in hurricane policy and that hurricane policy focuses more on preparedness, forecasting, warning, and evacuation than does earthquake policy by virtue of the very different mechanisms involved. We can also claim that the earthquake problem has been more successfully "federalized" than the hurricane problem has, even though the scope of the two problems is similar. This is because the scientific community has been more cohesive and persuasive in its claims that earthquake hazards require a significant federal role. This role is best exemplified by the National Earthquake Hazards Reduction Program, a large program that has existed far longer than the wind program, which was enacted only in 2004 as an add-on to the reauthorization of the earthquake program.

These conclusions are somewhat complicated by the different kinds of damage done by hurricanes and earthquakes. Officials concerned with the hurricane hazard must be concerned with the wind and flood hazards, both in the storm surge area and in inland flooding. Inland flooding was particularly severe in Hurricane Floyd and was the major cause of damage by Hurricane Hazel in 1954 and Hurricane Agnes in 1972. Earthquakes, by contrast, generally damage buildings.

In the case of earthquakes, the state-level focus has been on mitigation of the hazard through improved building code provisions. The major cause of injury and death in earthquakes is the failure of buildings, so the goal is to build structures in a way that they will, in current engineering parlance, "fail gracefully" (that is, be rendered unsuitable for future use but without killing people). This safety imperative is clear from the history of what states and localities choose to regulate. For example, Seattle has regulations for ensuring that parapets do not fall from buildings and hurt people standing under them; this regulation is the direct result of experience in the 1965 Seattle earthquake (May, Fox, and Hasan 1989). And California's earthquake policy history is essentially a story of stimulus and response. To the extent that Washington State has demonstrated any learning, it is for the most part vicariously and indirectly through California's experience and through the more advanced, California-driven seismic provisions of the Uniform Building Code, much of which has now been incorporated in the new International Building Code. There is therefore considerable evidence of instrumental policy learning in California and some evidence of it in Washington.

There is also evidence of instrumental policy learning in the two hurricane-prone states but, to a greater extent than in California's earthquakes, experience had to accumulate before aggressive action was ultimately taken. In hurricane-prone states, the risks of hurricanes are well known, so that attempts were made to incorporate this risk experience (which is somewhat different from direct disaster experience) in land-use planning, particularly through the NFIP.

Finally, it is important to consider the federal government's role in these processes. One might argue that California is the leader, and all the other states followers, in earthquake policy. But the federal government has played an important centralizing role, through the NEHRP, in collecting information, supporting research, and promoting improved mitigation at the state and local levels. Without this federal support, state-level efforts to mitigate earthquake hazards in other earthquake-prone states would probably be far less advanced than they are. This may not have been the original intention of the key legislative champion of the NEHRP, Senator Alan Cranston, whose interests were clearly focused on California. But by "federalizing" the earthquake hazard, the proponents of the NEHRP made resources available to other states with earthquake hazards. The lack of a substantial centralizing role for the federal government in hurricane policy means that states must rely more on themselves to develop and implement innovative hurricane mitigation policies that go beyond the usual solutions, such as floodwalls or changes in the building code. While the passage of the wind hazard program in 2004 was an attempt to create a federal role in hurricane policy parallel to its role in earthquake policy, the relatively small size of this program compared with the earthquake program means that change in hurricane mitigation policy is likely to remain distributed across the states.

Conclusions

The propositions outlined in chapter 1 assumed that at least some individual events lead to policy change. Indeed, in the model of event-related learning, an event is assumed to trigger some sort of legislative or regulatory activity through the mobilization of groups that promote policy innovations.

The history of the natural hazards domain suggests that at the national level, individual events, while they gain considerable attention and can have great value in setting agendas, do not appear to lead to direct change the way they have in aviation security and homeland security. Instead, the accumulation of experience influences policy change; learning is cumulative. Individual natural disasters do not appear to have much power to change policy because few groups mobilize in response to an event and explicitly lobby for policy change at the federal level. Nor does the range of issues change greatly in the wake of an event: the larger the disaster, the greater the demands for relief; these demands dominate the agenda and policymaking. Nor are events themselves linked to the "objective lessons" of the event, if we accept the emerging professional consensus (one challenged, however, within Congress and in parts of the emergency management community) that mitigation is a cost-effective way of preventing losses from future disasters.

Social and instrumental policy learning in any domain are long-term processes. Instrumental learning is manifest in legislative changes that emphasize mitigation of the hazards posed by natural disasters. In the area of social policy learning, governments at all levels, and some private individuals, have become aware that natural disasters are not merely acts of God about which nothing can be done but that steps can be taken to mitigate hazards. For example, California first enacted progressive engineering standards for public buildings after the 1933 Long Beach earthquake when it passed the Field Act, which required that schools be built to withstand earthquakes with minimal risk to human life and safety. After the 1971 San Fernando earthquake, the California legislature enacted the Alquist–Priolo Special Studies Zones Act, which required that local communities adjust land-use planning to account for seismicity and that they inform purchasers of land of their susceptibility to earthquakes. In this respect, as we have seen, California is a leader in the area of social policy learning about earthquakes and has taken much more aggressive action to mitigate hazards than has neighboring Washington State.

There is reason to believe that policymakers are coming to understand the causal factors involved in the damage and disruption done by a range of disasters, which is a necessary first step toward reducing damage and disruption. Repeated disasters help reinforce these lessons, as suggested by the passage of the Bunning-Bereuter-Blumenauer Flood Insurance Act of 2004 (PL 108-264, enacted June 30, 2004). For the first time, federal legislation recognized the problems involved in providing flood insurance to properties that repeatedly experience flood damage. The act addresses this problem by funding mitigation techniques ranging from structural building modifications to relocation away from flood-prone areas. This legislation is the result of years of experience with a very small number of properties that account for a large number of claims under the NFIP (Birkland et al. 2003; Conrad, Stout, and McNitt 1998).

Clearly, then, some learning is occurring about the tools available to mitigate hazards, but we cannot say that there is a direct relationship between disasters, experience, and improved policy. Features of the American political system and of the disasters themselves continue to retard the application of lessons learned about natural hazards. For one thing, response to natural disasters is generally a function of local government, and disaster preparedness and mitigation is not a high priority for local officials (Alesch and Petak 1986; 2001). For another thing, disaster relief, as opposed to mitigation, remains an extremely popular policy. Fifty years of efforts to coordinate and rationalize disaster policy have failed to account for the distributive nature of disaster relief in the United States. While Congress has long understood this, it was only during the Clinton administration—when professional disaster managers were put in charge of FEMA for the first time— that the White House learned of the political power of the presidential disaster declaration (Platt 1999, chapter 1). The debacle of FEMA's responses to Hurricane Hugo and in particular to Hurricane Andrew taught President Clinton the political value of quick and effective federal responses to disasters. Clinton declared more disasters than any other president ever had. Declarations of disaster trigger a flow of federal money for which members of Congress can claim credit. It is therefore unlikely that the system of disaster relief in the United States will change, except marginally, in the coming decades. Indeed, the failure to provide relief rapidly is still politically costly, as President Bush found after Hurricane Katrina. No president, on the other hand, has ever been politically damaged by failing to promote mitigation.

A third potential obstacle to learning in the future is the relocation of FEMA within the Department of Homeland Security, which has reduced FEMA's stature and its access to the president. The DHS is dominated by personnel with experience in law enforcement or national security, which, as Hurricane Katrina showed, is not transferable to responses to natural disasters (in addition, the usefulness of such experience in responding to terrorist attacks is questionable, at best) (Tierney 2005). Promoting hazard mitigation under this kind of leadership will be particularly challenging, especially when the organizational change at

FEMA is coupled with higher priority on homeland security and the Bush administration's neglect of or even antipathy toward hazard mitigation, as evidenced by its termination of Project Impact.

In the end, learning in the field of natural hazards is a function of experience, both in the actions of professionals whose training and expertise compel their involvement in policymaking and in political leaders who weigh the political costs and benefits of applying lessons to actual policy.

five

disaster, learning, and the possibility of change

One of the first things we learn as students of American public policy is that significant policy change is difficult to achieve in our constitutional system. The barriers placed in the way of meaningful change are often formidable, and they include long-standing cultural and ideological obstacles to action, as well as institutional and constitutional rules that favor "deliberation" or "delay" (depending on one's taste) over rapid response and action. While some may complain about the pace of policy change, others actually find barriers to change, and the stability this promotes, a positive good. The federal system, the separation of powers, and the rules of the legislative branch that seek to promote both majority rule and minority rights are held up as brilliant features of the founders' constitutional design. One can certainly argue that these features have made the United States one of the world's most stable political systems, even if it is also subject to considerable stasis and resistance to change (Robertson and Judd 1989).

Despite the many barriers to rapid action and policy change, these things do in fact occur. Change is most discernible when one studies policymaking over periods of ten years or more

(Sabatier 1993). The United States today is not the same nation it was in 1789, 1932, or even 1980. Social, economic, and technological changes exert pressure on government to harness change, adapt to it, or regulate its undesirable effects. Economists and policy analysts often call for government action in cases of market failure. Pollution control, for example, is an attempt to capture in the costs of goods the negative externalities that are borne by people who may not consume the goods. In the last chapter we saw how taxpayers subsidize the federal flood insurance program—a central feature of hurricane policy—because no insurance company will create a private market for flood insurance. In other cases social norms change over time; in one hundred years the United States went from legalized slavery, to legalized segregation, to outlawing segregation, to adopting affirmative action policies intended to overcome the legacy of slavery and racism. Many would argue that our nation has yet to achieve full racial and ethnic equality, but few would deny that the nation has made progress over the past hundred years, even if that progress has been slow.

While the American system is slow and deliberative by design, rapid policy change in the face of major focusing events is possible, as the previous chapters have illustrated. In cases such as the terrorist attacks of September 11, 2001, change would not have happened to the same extent or at the same pace without the catalytic effect of the event. At the same time, such events demonstrate that the system can harness existing ideas to address the problems and failures revealed by a focusing event. Sometimes a natural disaster inspires a major policy review. In other cases, major policy changes may not occur until years later.

This chapter reviews the role of learning in the process of policymaking. This discussion provides the context for an assessment of the individual elements of the learning model depicted in the first chapter and of factors that promote and inhibit learning. The discussion concludes with a look at Hurricane Katrina, which helps us understand how lessons get "unlearned." Hurricane Katrina, like other disasters, is an example of the difference between a lesson "observed" and a lesson "learned."

Learning and the Policy Process

I have argued in the previous pages and elsewhere that focusing events elevate problems on the policy agenda. My definition of the term "focusing event" relies heavily on a dramatic increase in mass and elite attention. In Kingdon's streams model of the policy-making process, a focusing event opens a "window of opportunity" for change, in which various "streams" come together. In my model, a focusing event may influence the policy stream by drawing attention to ideas that were generally unformulated before the event, and may create the opportunity for a new look at policies previously considered politically unpalatable or unnecessary.

A focusing event can also influence the problem stream, because it may change our understanding of how and why problems come about. In an extreme case, an event might influence the politics stream, though this will usually not become clear until the next election cycle, which can be years distant; in the intervening time, memories of the event can fade as other issues take precedence. Disasters, however, can cause politicians to lose elections, particularly at the local level. Nearly everyone has heard stories of mayors who failed to win re-election because they were slow to remove snow from the streets after a blizzard. However, while speculation surrounded the political fates of New Orleans mayor Ray Nagin and Louisiana governor Kathleen Blanco after their allegedly inept response to Hurricane Katrina, Nagin was able, very narrowly, to win re-election against a strong opponent. Both these examples are anecdotal and are largely concerned with the electoral outcomes of focusing events. Such effects have proved very difficult to measure.

Policy process theories, by contrast, give us a theoretical framework for understanding the policy implications of focusing events. The policy process literature suggests that we should be very cautious about attributing policy change to any one cause. A first principle of any theory of policy change is that focusing events do not automatically bring it about. Indeed, this must be the default position, because so few events really have a discernible influence on policy in the immediate aftermath of the event. Sometimes the event is simply insufficiently compelling to yield policy change.

Look at the 2004 hurricane season, and at Hurricane Ivan in particular, which yielded no changes in the building code for buildings more than one mile inland in the Florida Panhandle. Even in the face of the 2004 storms, and with memories of Hurricanes Katrina and Wilma still fresh, Florida has not yet adopted stringent building standards in the Panhandle. In other cases, the window of opportunity may close before policy change can occur. We can say, however, that most focusing events will open the window of opportunity for policy change, which is another way of saying that focusing events make policy change more likely. Policy theorists treat these events—and the probability of change—somewhat differently in their models of the policy process, but the results are similar.

According to Frank Baumgartner and Bryan Jones, a focusing event may draw attention to an issue, usually negative attention. Policies, the assumptions behind them, and their advocates are called into question as attention becomes more intense. In some cases members of the "policy monopoly" may lose control of the "policy image" that dominates the domain. For example, Baumgartner and Jones (1993) found that the nuclear power monopoly broke down over time as events and political changes came together to allow greater participation in nuclear energy issues by environmental groups that had previously found it very difficult to gain access to the policy community (see also Birkland 1997a, chapter 5).

Paul Sabatier's advocacy coalition framework has clearly influenced my thinking on the organization of policy communities (Sabatier and Jenkins-Smith 1993). Sabatier argues that most policy domains are not composed of dozens of separate groups but of two to four advocacy coalitions that form around a set of shared beliefs. However, as we have seen, natural hazards policy is a "policy without a public," largely the province of technical experts inside government and expert communities of engineers or scientists (May 1990). In a similar way, government experts are most clearly involved in making aviation security policy, with the participation of other "in-group" representatives such as airport operators or airlines. Like natural disasters, aviation security is a policy without a public, although the aviation domain looks much more like the earthquake domain than the hurricane domain. As with earthquakes, decision making in aviation security is largely the province of technical experts, although there appear to be two advocacy coalitions, one for the airlines and one for federal aviation regulators. By contrast, there is so little evidence of mobilization on the part of experts to promote solutions to the hurricane hazard that we can say that there is no advocacy coalition in this domain; rather, hurricane policy, to the extent it exists, is largely about distributing disaster relief to affected areas. At best, we can say that hurricane policy is embedded in a broader "disaster policy domain," in which some, but not much, attention is paid to hazard mitigation.

Revisiting the Propositions

This background on the policy process, the nature of agenda setting, and the organization of policy domains provides a foundation for understanding two key issues to which we shall now turn. The first is to what extent the model introduced in chapter 1 is a sound depiction of event-centered policy change, of which learning is a key component. The second concerns the factors that promote or impede learning from disasters.

A Small Number of Events Will Gain the Most Attention

It is simple enough to plot the number of news stories about an event, or to list the number of witnesses who testify before Congress about a recent event. These measures allow us to find spikes in media and legislative attention to relatively few events. While Congress and the news media may take brief notice of smaller events—minor earthquakes, for example, or small security breaches—the "largest" events, those that do the greatest damage, gain the most attention. Thus the September 11 attacks received far more attention than the TWA and Pan Am crashes, but these events gained greater attention than lesser aviation security incidents that preceded them.

Some events get a lot of attention both because they are objectively large and because their impact is so great that they almost invariably reveal some sort of policy failure. In the case of

September 11, the policy failures are well known. Hurricane Andrew revealed the inability of FEMA to respond quickly to a large natural disaster while also revealing failures in state and local building code enforcement; thirteen years later, Hurricane Katrina revealed some of the same problems at FEMA. The Loma Prieta and Northridge earthquakes revealed that the changes to construction practices that followed the 1971 San Fernando earthquake were either incompletely implemented or were insufficient in the face of larger earthquakes.

The paradox of learning driven by truly large events is that whereas such events provide significant fodder for learning, they are also likely to overwhelm the ability of a system to respond with routine procedures and therefore may limit learning. Large events are exceptions rather than typical examples of the problems in a given domain. One could argue that in domains prone to disasters large events are the most important from a learning perspective because they reveal just how bad a disaster can be. As noted earlier, Lee Clarke (2005a) argues that small events are unlikely to yield "possibilistic" or "worst-case" thinking that will drive action. Small events are more likely to be explained away as the normal sort of variation in program performance that one would expect in any complex system. When a passenger is discovered with a weapon on an airliner but without criminal intent, the aviation security system is deemed able to address this problem without requiring legislative change. Many weapons have inadvertently been carried onto aircraft both before and after the September 11 attacks, but they were not considered sufficiently serious as to require policy change. Indeed, the detection of weapons since September 11 has been cited as proof that the new screening procedures work. Security breaches involving the hijacking or bombing of an airplane, by contrast, are obviously much more serious. These events therefore gain considerable attention and are likely to open the window of opportunity for policy change much wider, and for a longer period of time, than would less visible and dramatic events.

Attention, therefore, may be as much a function of the "size" of an event in a scientific sense as a function of the consequences of the event. The size and importance of an event are socially constructed, but the event has to come first, and it has to be large enough to attract attention (measured by number of people killed, geographical extent of damage, value of property damage, etc.). If the event is large enough by one or more of these measurements, it is likely to trigger debate over how it should be understood, or constructed. Hurricane Katrina got a lot of attention for affecting a large number of people. Only after the storm was over did debate begin over whether the damage was as bad as it was because FEMA failed to plan, or because state and local governments were inept, or because of racial and income stratification, or because of the development of coastal wetlands, or because Congress hadn't given the Corps of Engineers enough money to fix the levees. These arguments were a consequence of the attention paid to the event because of its size, not the cause.

Large events are more likely than small ones to trigger discussion of a broad range of problems. For example, the Columbine High School shooting in Colorado in 1999 was the largest single act of school violence in the United States in terms of the number of people killed and injured. Columbine and similar but smaller school shootings in Oregon, Arkansas, and elsewhere broadened the scope of debate over the causes of school violence.

In the same way, the September 11 attacks opened up two overlapping domains to a wide range of ideas: the homeland security domain and the aviation safety domain. Before September 11, the two most recent major security breaches focused official attention on bombs. The September 11 hijackings turned attention to improving passenger screening, reinforcing cockpit doors, allowing flight crews to carry weapons, and other security innovations. At the same time, the attacks caused policymakers and the media to pay attention to a much broader range of issues, among them immigration reform and border controls, bioterrorism, port security, and cybersecurity, to name just a few. In short, large events provoke consideration of a wide range of issues because they open up much more agenda space than smaller, more routine events, allowing more ideas to emerge and compete.

The implications for domains with a large number of small events are clear: Small events will lead to the discussion of a narrow range of issues, if issues are discussed at all. Learning from any particular disaster is usually possible only if it is of a sufficient size to gain attention in the first place. If a domain is characterized by a series of small events, policymaking is likely to resemble what happens when many small events (say, car accidents) indicate a problem (say, poorly lit roads).

Focusing Events Trigger Group Mobilization

If a focusing event triggers claims of policy failure, one might assume that a broad range of groups will mobilize to press for reform. Indeed, this is what happened after the *Exxon Valdez* oil spill, when the environmental movement mobilized to lobby for substantial revisions to federal laws regarding liability for oil spills and responsibility for their cleanup (Birkland 1997a, chapter 4). In the domains addressed in this book, however, mobilization occurs among a much narrower group of actors. As we have seen, all four domains engage "policies without publics."

This finding raises a set of questions. First, did I inadvertently select only policies without publics, thereby excluding policy domains with more "publics"? Or are all domains that are prone to disasters equally likely to lack organized interest groups? It is likely that disaster-prone domains are more like "policies without publics" than they are like domains that inspire interest group mobilization. But other domains may show traditional interest group mobilization triggered or enhanced by a recent event. Two obvious domains that come to mind are the oil spill domain and nuclear power domain. In the oil spill domain, the *Exxon Valdez* oil spill mobilized interest groups and concomitantly demobilized the oil industry, as measured by the types of witnesses who appeared before congressional committees. Similar results were found for the nuclear power domain, although with respect to oil spills, oil companies were much less likely to testify about specific spills than were environmental groups and their allies. In the nuclear power domain, by contrast, the extreme level of political polarization as well as the ambiguous outcome of the Three Mile Island accident, which has not demonstrably killed or injured anyone, made industry representatives just as likely to talk about a specific event as environmental groups were. The important finding in both domains, however, is the existence of groups that could make a sound claim to be representing the public interest.

There is nothing to suggest that the process of learning or policy change will necessarily be different because of the presence of particular kinds of mobilized interest groups. What is most important is the extent to which ideas are mobilized, either by groups representing the public interest or by government officials or technical experts. It is in fact plausible to argue that most policy will engage relatively few "publics," except perhaps for client groups in the policy domain, such as farm interests in farm policy, or defense contractors in military procurement policy. Policy typologies advanced by Theodore Lowi (1964) and James Q. Wilson (1973) suggest that only the most visible policies that impose direct costs on particular interests will yield broad-based mobilization.

In any case, as we have seen, most of the hard work of generating new policy ideas in these domains falls to technical experts both within and outside government. This claim is a fit subject for future research. For now we can say that there is little evidence to support the proposition that group mobilization will be accompanied by an increased discussion of policy ideas, if we are talking about groups that previously had trouble finding an audience for their argument. Rather, a focusing event itself, without the intervention of interest groups, causes the same actors that dominated policymaking before the event to consider ideas more intensively than they did before.

The Relationship between Events, Ideas, and Policy Change

The fourth proposition in chapter 1 held that there is a relationship between ideas and policy change and that, in particular, change is more likely when ideas are triggered by events than when they are not. The literature on which this study draws broadly agrees that policy change is the function of ideas, and this study argues that new ideas are not developed in response to an event. Instead, focusing events tend to reinvigorate attention to preexisting ideas. This is entirely consistent with the advocacy coalition, streams, and punctuated equilibrium models of the policy process discussed in chapter 1.

Three findings of this study support this proposition. The first is that there are very few novel problems and solutions; rather, focusing events direct attention to existing problems. Second, focusing events can create a presumption in favor of policy change. Third, learning can be said to have occurred when the proximate causes of the policy failure revealed by the event are subsequently addressed by changes in policy.

Very Few Problems Are Entirely New

The September 11 attacks struck many people, including those in government and other positions of authority, as entirely novel events. In fact, while the use of airplanes to destroy buildings was new to most policymakers, journalists, and the public at large, experts in aviation security had considered the possibility of this sort of terrorism.

Had September 11 been evidence of an entirely novel problem, policymakers could not have taken a number of ideas off the shelf and enacted them as policy. Indeed, instrumental learning had been occurring before September 11. Many if not most of the ideas implemented after the September 11 attacks were already on the agenda, although they were well known primarily only to experts. As discussed in chapter 1, the idea for a Department of Homeland Security or a similar agency predates the September 11 attacks. Other aspects of current antiterrorism policy are "spillovers," as Kingdon would call them, from other policy domains. For example, the inability of the Immigration and Naturalization Service (INS) to track foreign visitors, efficiently manage student and other types of visas, and prevent significant numbers of illegal immigrants from entering the United States, primarily from Mexico, has been well known to policymakers for years. The INS and its border patrol functions were not reformed, however, because the problem was not sufficiently urgent and because economic interests such as agriculture rely on undocumented immigrants for a large part of their workforce. September 11 changed that by prompting the absorption of key functions of the INS into the newly created Department of Homeland Security.

Nor are there many, if any, truly novel events in the natural hazards domain. The size of an event is considered most noteworthy; there are relatively few truly catastrophic natural disasters, which is why we call them low-probability/high-consequence events.

Learning in the natural hazards domain accumulates over time from many events. For example, the National Earthquake Hazards Reduction Act was not the direct consequence of any one earthquake. The soil was fertile for such legislation because of many factors, including the experience of the 1964 Alaska and 1971 San Fernando earthquakes, a huge earthquake in China that killed well over half a million people and injured well over half a million more, and the efforts of a policy entrepreneur—Senator Alan Cranston—who saw the value of this program for his earthquake-prone state. Similarly, the Stafford Act and the Disaster Management Act of 2000 were products of years of accumulated experience with natural hazards.

Because there are few entirely new problems, focusing events cause preexisting policy ideas to be revamped. Rather than spur innovation, disasters allow proponents of particular policy options to advance their ideas, usually at the expense of other ideas. For example, after the Pan Am 103 and TWA 800 crashes, companies that made explosives-detection equipment seized the opportunity to promote the sale of particular technologies for detecting explosives, and to suggest that explosives detection—not passenger screening or manual screening of bags—was the most fruitful way to improve aviation security.

September 11 and its aftermath may be the clearest example of the repackaging of previously existing proposals across a range of areas in response to one event. There had long been simmering discontentment with the handling of both illegal immigrants and airline security before September 11, and the terrorist attacks changed both the statutory authorities and the organization of these governmental functions. September 11 provided an opportunity for politically conservative, pro–law enforcement groups to pass legislation that significantly increased the power of law enforcement in areas such as wiretapping. Indeed, "wiretapping" is an obsolete term for the range of powers that the government now has under the Patriot Act to perform surveillance of a wide range of communications. Moreover, the September 11 attacks ultimately elevated the idea of "homeland security"—a term previously familiar only to policy wonks—to the highest level of national politics and public consciousness. Yet the creation of the DHS was based largely on the recommendations of one report, that of the

Hart–Rudman Commission; in other words, September 11 did not change the knowledge base appreciably. What changed were political actors' motivations to act and to use whatever tools were at hand to respond to a threat that had suddenly become more apparent, if not greater in a true probabilistic sense, with the September 11 attacks.

Focusing Events and the Presumption against Change

The sort of barriers to learning and policy change that Peter May identifies are generally associated with periods of "normal politics," in which important issues may not be salient, facts tend to be contested, and change, when it happens at all, is marginal. Focusing events change the salience of issues and sometimes replace indicator-based analyses with much more emotionally charged examples of policy failure and the need for reform.

There is clear evidence that the orientation of aviation security was at least temporarily disrupted by the three aviation security events considered in this study. After all three of these events, major commissions were set up to study what went wrong and to put systems in place to prevent a recurrence. The creation of these commissions is evidence of the shift in favor of some sort of change, even as we acknowledge that substantive change will not be automatic.

A similar sense that change was necessary motivated actors in the homeland security domain, and a number of new laws were passed to address the wide range of issues brought to light by the September 11 attacks. The attacks were considerably different from earlier events, both in the aviation security and homeland security domains, in that very rapid action followed the event. No commissions were created or studies called for by Congress or the president in the immediate wake of September 11. Rather, legislation was passed almost immediately. In the space of one year, significant new law enforcement powers were enacted, new agencies were created, and esoteric aspects of homeland security such as cybersecurity became issues of widespread public interest.

Learning from natural disasters is subtler. No single disaster seems to create a presumption in favor of major change. Rather, major changes like the enactment of the Stafford Act come some time after several major disasters have occurred. This delay does not mean that no efforts are made to promote learning, of course. In the earthquake domain, there is considerable evidence of organized efforts to learn from every earthquake, regardless of where in the world it strikes. The event itself may not yield much pressure for policy change; the accumulation of knowledge takes place over time, largely without public pressure or participation.

Causes, Objective Lessons, and Learning

Learning from a disaster should be straightforward: An event happens, a policy failure is revealed, hearings are held about this failure, and policy changes, whether regulatory or statutory, are adopted to prevent the failure from recurring.

This sequence has largely been the history of aviation security in the United States. While the threats have not been responded to as quickly as some might have liked, it is now more difficult—not impossible, but more difficult—to hijack or bomb airliners in the United States. This tightening of a gap may induce terrorists to attempt other means, such as chemical or biological weapons or more traditional truck bombs, to achieve their goals. Indeed, regulators and lawmakers acknowledged this possibility when they took additional measures to protect ports and devoted some resources to the threat of terrorism on trains and other transportation systems. Here is another example of spillovers to policy domains; these ancillary changes might also be the unintended consequences of improved aviation security.

Learning is somewhat more complex in the natural hazards domain because the links between the natural phenomenon, the human adjustment to the phenomenon, and the improved policies are not as clear as they could be. In particular, the two related difficulties that continue to plague policy-oriented learning in natural hazards are the perceived inability of policy to do much about a hazard (the "act of God" problem) and the perceived low salience of the issue among most local officials. It falls to the federal government to set policy, and it takes more time and more events across the nation to accumulate the experience needed to change national policy.

There is also an entrenched belief that the system for dealing with hazards works fine just the way it is. This may well be true in the case of political actors. Members of Congress strongly favor disaster relief programs because they allow politicians to bring home the political bacon at virtually no political cost to any member, save for the usual quid pro quos when other spending bills come up. Since 1992 and the debacle of Hurricane Andrew, the executive branch has learned that it can make major political gains from the timely delivery of disaster relief to areas struck by earthquakes, hurricanes, floods, and even blizzards or other forms of severe weather that used to be taken for granted as normal facts of life.

In the general area of terrorism policy, instrumental learning as a direct result of objective "lessons" is hard to detect. If the only response to the September 11 attacks had been the correction of flaws directly revealed by the attack, policy change would have been limited to improved aviation security, more stringent immigration restrictions, better intelligence gathering and information sharing, and so on. But the spectacular nature of the September 11 attacks increased public awareness of the terrorist threat to such a degree that scenarios such as the poisoning of a municipal water supply, the use of a "dirty bomb," or the introduction of a plant or animal pathogen into American agriculture are now seen as possible or even likely. Still, few of the policy responses to September 11 fall into the realm of instrumental learning. Rather, we can see evidence of social policy learning in the social construction of the terrorist threat more broadly, and of political learning about the palatability of strong federal law enforcement powers in a "time of war." As noted earlier, there was almost no attempt to study the terrorist problem or to use "after-action reports" to shape post–September 11 policy. Instead policy proceeded without reference to studies or other attempts to learn systematically how to address the terrorist threat.

Assessing the Elements of the Model

The model of event-related learning depicted in figure 1.2 (chapter 1) strongly suggests that elements of the model should occur in order. First there is a focusing event, then group mobilization, then idea mobilization, then the translation of new ideas into policy. While this is a useful way of categorizing and ordering the various aspects of learning from focusing events, the model suffers from the usual problems of any model ordered temporally, such as the policy process model itself. The model assumes that one stage happens after another and that one stage must necessarily occur before the following one can occur. The reality is not quite so neat.

In the case studies examined in this book, we saw that specific events, unsurprisingly, drew attention to the issues of earthquakes, hurricanes, homeland security, and aviation security. This attention is assumed to yield group mobilization in one of two ways: Either groups troubled by an event mobilize to press for policy change, or groups see an opportunity to capitalize on the negative policy image of the domain that the event triggers.

As we have seen, this mobilization does not necessarily occur. We certainly cannot say that earthquakes and hurricanes yield broad-based, grassroots group mobilization. Nor is there much evidence of this sort of mobilization in the realm of homeland security. Policymaking in the domains considered in this study tends to be dominated by technical experts rather than by social movements or public interest groups. Unlike environmental disasters, which tend to galvanize environmental activists, the events described in this study have little or no mobilizing effect on groups that claim to represent the broader public interest. We can therefore modify the model somewhat to suggest that some category of advocates for policy change will be mobilized by focusing events. When the event mobilizes those inside government, or in a privileged position in the policy domain, we call this "inside mobilization" (Cobb, Ross, and Ross 1976).

What is not entirely clear from this study is to what extent ideas about the causes of problems (which lead to social policy learning) or ideas about policy tools (which lead to instrumental policy learning) would be generated without the mobilization of groups or individual "inside" advocates. Regardless of the nature of the mobilization, ideas clearly arise in the immediate aftermath of a focusing event and form the building blocks of subsequent policy change. The model can accommodate the idea that group mobilization leads to the promotion of ideas, or that an event merely increases attention to policy ideas that already existed and then became more widely known through the actions of enterprising journalists or the activities of policy entrepreneurs or advocates.

The final step of the model is actual policy change. I measured policy change in this study by the adoption of actual legislation, but this is a particularly stringent standard. Regulatory change is also evidence of policy change, and where appropriate I have referenced this in the case studies. There is little evidence that focusing events lead to regulatory change at the federal level. There is, however, qualitative evidence that disasters can influence state and local regulations such as building codes. And in aviation security there is evidence of some regulatory change after dramatic events—for example, the FAA's requirement after the September 11 attacks that cockpit doors be secured throughout all phases of flight. This study does little to detect whether and to what extent "standard operating procedures" or the actions of "street-level bureaucrats" change after a focusing event. For example, after September 11, passenger screeners at airports became more vigilant in their searches for newly prohibited items. In a similar way, members of the public learn more about the things they can do at home to mitigate natural hazards. While not a "policy" change per se, this sort of behavioral change is generally desirable and can be exploited by policymakers to encourage individual efforts to make people safer.

Factors That Promote and Inhibit Learning

The first proposition introduced in chapter 1—that most if not all participants in a policy domain want to solve the problems revealed by a focusing event—suggests that focusing events promote efforts to learn. This does not mean that there won't be very different ideas about how to solve a problem, or even how to define it. In the case of flooding caused by hurricanes, some will argue that people shouldn't build their houses so close to the beach, whereas others will argue that homes can be built on the beach if building codes are altered to make them more storm worthy. In the case of aviation security, some will argue that security is a cost of doing business that should be borne by airlines, whereas others will argue that aviation security is a national security matter best managed by the federal government. Regardless of these inevitable disagreements, most participants want to promote some sort of problem solving. A focusing event promotes learning because people are motivated to address the problems revealed by the event.

Factors That Promote Learning

One of the assumptions behind my research was that existing mechanisms for learning are present in certain policy domains and that their presence promotes instrumental policy learning. The results of this study suggest that media attention, particularly to highly salient issues, promotes learning. Organizational features of the policy domain will promote or inhibit learning. Domains in which ideas for improved policy have accumulated over time are more likely to show evidence of instrumental learning than are those domains in which this experience does not accumulate.

Media Attention

Media attention to public problems, and to a lesser extent to proposed solutions, promotes learning. Social policy learning is advanced when particular social constructions of problems become dominant in media coverage. The news media provide rapid feedback to those who seek to construct problems in particular ways or to reinforce those constructions. In the disaster field, people harmed by natural phenomena are often considered "disaster victims," even if their losses resulted in part because they failed to take active steps to protect their lives and property, such as purchasing flood insurance, or because they knowingly assumed a risk that could have been avoided, such as building a house on a beach. Constructing those who lose their lives or property as "victims" who unwittingly suffered at the hand of nature leads almost inevitably to demands for "relief" for these individuals. As Deborah Stone has noted, these "causal stories" have a powerful influence on the nature of the debate over policies and therefore on the shape of policy itself (Stone 1989, 2002). Were the news media to emphasize the need for hazard mitigation rather than relief, one might assume that policy would similarly reflect the importance of mitigation.

Media attention also promotes political learning because the media report what political tactics succeed or fail in advancing an argument and influencing policy. Without media coverage, participants in political discourse might not know to what extent their arguments are influencing policymaking. Much of American political debate is conducted not behind closed doors but through the news media. Participants in policy debates quickly learn what sort of political arguments reporters will focus on and which will be ignored. Thus a large part of political learning concerns how to make an argument that will be persuasive to both the public and to the reporters who serve as gatekeepers of the political agenda. Focusing events increase the chances that arguments about policy failure revealed by the event will gain attention.

Baumgartner and Jones argue that opportunities for policy change emerge when greater attention is paid to issues. If change is about learning, then we can assume that attention leads to efforts to learn, which leads to efforts to change policy. Because actual policymaking is often highly technical, however, policy learning is not directly influenced by media coverage. Rather, pressure to "do something" accompanies events, which then leads to efforts to adapt existing ideas to the new situation. Thus instrumental learning follows greater attention. This may explain why the policymakers John Kingdon interviewed claimed not to be greatly influenced by media coverage.

Salience

Related to media attention is the question of salience. A salient issue is an issue that is very important to the public and to policymakers, or is potentially important to them under the right circumstances. A salient issue gains attention, and attention can often yield policy change. However, such policy change can be the result of learning, mimicking, or mere pressure to act; change by itself is not evidence of learning from an event. Media coverage is a rough measure of salience but does not tell the whole story. Focusing events elevate dormant issues to salience. As noted in chapter 2, in the two years before September 11 "terrorism" was not listed among the "most important problems" cited by respondents to the Gallup Poll. After September 11, terrorism was cited as the third-most important problem in many polls, after the perennial favorites, jobs and the economy.

Large disasters can make nearly any issue salient, at least for a while. Extensive media coverage of hurricanes and earthquakes will raise public concern about these hazards, but salience does not necessarily correlate with improved public understanding of the problem or a better sense of what government can reasonably do about it. The record of congressional hearings suggests that the public may well see hurricanes as a prominent issue, but their concerns focus largely on disaster relief and recovery. Recovery is often defined as a return to the status quo, even when the event revealed that the status quo placed people and property at risk. One should not, however, make too much of public perceptions of the problem. As my case studies show, policy advocates can use public concern about an event to pressure policymakers to adopt reforms, particularly at the state level. Indeed, hazards professionals know that one of the best times to promote mitigation is when memories of the current disaster are fresh. This impetus for promoting mitigation sometimes runs up against public opposition to certain mitigation measures, such as retreat from the coastline or floodplain or costly structural retrofitting. Still, the point is not whether mitigation measures are wholly adopted after a natural disaster but whether a disaster makes the issue sufficiently salient to warrant discussion, thereby increasing the chances for policy change. Focusing events clearly make these issues more salient. Moreover, there is evidence that policy change is a result of the increased attention that follows disasters. Some of this policy change is clearly the result of pressure to "do something" after an event, particularly when failing to act would seem to reflect a lack of compassion for the victims of a disaster. But the accumulation of experience with disasters also has led to real efforts to understand why disasters occur and how policies can be crafted to minimize their effects.

Policy Domain Organization

It appears that the presence of at least one major advocacy coalition in a policy domain has an important influence on the likelihood of learning from disasters. This is most aptly illustrated in the hurricane domain, where at the national level, programs to learn about hurricane hazards and to apply that learning to improving preparedness and mitigation are much less important than they are in the earthquake domain. The earthquake domain has an organized policy community that presses government to do more to mitigate the earthquake hazard, which helps explain the relationships between events and policy change at the national level. Because there is no cohesive advocacy coalition at the national level in hurricane policy, pressure to learn from and mitigate hurricanes is much less pronounced at the national level. We have seen that public and private officials at the local level in North Carolina and Florida were able to press for policy change, but it is unclear whether this pressure has the same kind of enduring character that pressure from earthquake policy advocates has had for more than thirty years.

There are obvious advocacy coalitions in the aviation security domain. The dominant ones involve aviation security and safety advocates in Congress, in some agencies, and in the private realm on one side, and the airlines and their allies on the other. For years the airlines sought to thwart or delay more stringent aviation security procedures, claiming that they were unnecessary in the United States or were too costly in light of the actual risks. As a result, before September 11, 2001, baggage was not matched to passengers on each flight, few air marshals boarded flights, and security depended on a patchwork of private security firms whose hiring and training standards were found, even before September 11, to be woefully inadequate. Charges of policy failure were made by what we might call the security coalition, but such charges were only partially acted upon after Pan Am 103 and TWA 800. Policymakers took comprehensive action after September 11. The relative scarcity of advocates of more stringent security measures before September 11, compared with the lobbying power of the airline industry, made reform unlikely. But, thanks to these advocates, the ideas for improving aviation security were already on the shelf when the shortcomings of the system were dramatically revealed on September 11, which allowed the rapid adoption of new policies in response to the terrorist attacks.

Although the homeland security domain lacked the same kind of cohesive advocacy coalitions for and against increased national security before September 11, there was a similar debate between those who wanted increased security (expanded law enforcement powers, more stringent immigration and border controls, etc.), on the one hand, and those who believed that such measures would compromise civil liberties and other virtues of the American political system, on the other. The September 11 attacks lent the pro–national security advocates such power that they were able to overcome opposition to controversial legislation like the Patriot Act. These advocates could plausibly claim to represent the national interest against the particularistic claims of advocates in "smaller" domains.

Impediments to Learning

Peter May, in his analysis of several case studies of potential policy learning, found two impediments to learning. The first is "confusion over what it takes to improve policy performance." The second is a situation where "knowledge for improving policy performance exists, but policy makers are constrained by political or other factors in their abilities to incorporate such change in policy redesign." Furthermore, May argues, "the main barrier to social policy learning for many issues in American politics is the intense conflict and polarization of beliefs among competing advocacy coalitions" (May 1992, 349). "[B]roader forces in American politics than policy domain-specific changes in belief systems or new understandings of causal mechanisms have tended to dominate policy change" (352).

The political constraints on policymakers are part of the inherent bias in favor of the status quo. I have argued elsewhere that focusing events shift the presumption away from stasis and in favor of policy change. The *Exxon Valdez* oil spill, for example, broke a fourteen-year deadlock between opposing sides on the issues of response to and liability for oil spills. Similarly, the September 11 hijackings led to a shift in attitudes about who should be responsible for providing security in the passenger airline system. Aviation security moved from a question of transportation security to a question of national security, particularly when we learned that airplanes could be used as guided missiles, killing many more people than just those on the plane. This construction of aviation security as national security was not new, but September 11 provided the impetus for policy change.

But not all focusing events teach policymakers the "right" lessons. Rather, they can choose the least technically difficult policy options, options that promise the least political opposition, or both. Taking passenger screening away from the airlines and giving it to the federal government was neither technically challenging nor politically costly. Indeed, given the documented poor performance of private screening companies before September 11—a problem that the FAA was, in its plodding way, seeking to address through regulation—the decision to "federalize" screeners was not terribly difficult to make.

On the other hand, even large-scale natural disasters may fail to inspire effective hazard mitigation policies. The absence an advocacy coalition on hurricanes is a function both of "confusion over what it takes to improve policy performance" and of political constraints that prevent officials from adopting effective policies. The accumulation of hurricane experience over time may lead to incremental changes, such as the Flood Insurance Reform Act of 2004, but it is unlikely to spur the broad implementation of politically unpopular measures, such as banning home construction on the coastline. A particularly formidable obstacle to thoroughgoing reform is the tendency to treat disasters as opportunities to show "compassion" rather than to make hard choices. Most legislation that follows in the wake of natural disasters provides disaster relief and promotes recovery. On November 10, 2005, I searched the Library of Congress's Thomas database for legislation containing the word "Katrina." Of the 293 items this search returned, 48 percent of the bills mentioned Hurricane Katrina in the title, 24 percent included the word "relief" in the title, and the terms "recovery" and "reconstruction" were mentioned in 9 and 5 percent of the titles, respectively. The word "preparedness" appeared in three bills (1 percent), and the word "mitigation" did not appear in any bill. Clearly, mitigation or even preparedness was not a major concern of Congress in the two months after this disaster.[1]

Learning is also impeded by confusion about the nature and meaning of various events. Terrorist attacks throughout the 1990s led to considerable confusion about whether our response should take the form of revamped law enforcement efforts or military action, a question that became the subject of public debate, through the media, after the September 11 attacks. The variable and somewhat amorphous nature of terrorism compounded this confusion: Was the terrorist threat going to come primarily from disaffected Americans like Timothy McVeigh, or from international groups like al-Qaeda? Was terrorism sponsored by states, tolerated by states, or stateless? The lack of clear answers to such questions created significant barriers to learning—and therefore to policy change—in the domain of terrorism. Only the September 11 events brought sufficient clarity to allow the adoption of major counterterrorism policies. In this case, considerable social policy learning was necessary before instrumental policy learning could occur.

Two important research questions for the future are, first, whether social policy learning must precede instrumental policy learning, and, second, whether social policy lessons lead policymakers to prefer one solution to another. In the September 11 case the social policy lesson that appears to have been learned is that terrorism is more than a crime to be addressed in the criminal courts; rather, it is also an act of war that requires a military response. The shift from constructing terrorism as a crime to constructing it as national security problem substantially changed the nature and substance of the tools used to address terrorism. To be sure, many advocates of a proactive approach to terrorism had long argued that terrorism was a national security problem, and that the growing likelihood of WMD attacks and mass-casualty terrorism warranted this shift in thinking. But to the extent that this shift in thinking about terrorism was occurring before September 11, it was the attack itself rather than cumulative evidence that led to wholesale rethinking.

Focusing Events and the Accumulation of Knowledge

The cumulative nature of learning is clear, but its importance deserves further exploration. As noted above, the model of learning from focusing events suggests that if an event yields increased attention in agenda-setting terms, if it mobilizes advocates for change, and if it energizes a discussion of ideas related to the causes and solutions of the problem revealed by the event, then it is likely that event-related learning has occurred. I have modified this model somewhat to accommodate the idea that learning can happen without group mobilization. By definition, focusing events will draw attention to a problem; therefore increased attention is a necessary, but not sufficient, condition for event-related policy change.

At the heart of the model is the assumption that policy change and learning are linked in time with an event that can be said to have precipitated the learning. In many cases, however, a major event produces minor policy change or none at all. After the bombing of Pan Am 103 in 1988, the FAA created an office that dealt with terrorist threats to civil aviation but did not require more stringent baggage matching, explosives detection, or other tools. These tools reentered the policy debate after September 11, despite the fact that September 11 revealed problems in passenger screening rather than in baggage and bomb detection. But the loss of Pan Am 103 and then the loss of TWA 800 became important milestones in the history of aviation security. These events triggered some degree of policy change, but they were also important because they generated ideas that could be put into service after the September 11 attacks (Birkland 2004).

Cumulative learning may be even more important in the domain of natural hazards for two reasons. First, experience of a particular kind of disaster in one place can influence responses to the same kind of disaster elsewhere. In 2005 an earthquake off the coast of northern California led to tsunami warnings along the Oregon and California coasts. Tsunami warnings were of particular interest in June 2005 because of fresh memories of the December 26, 2004, tsunami in the Indian Ocean, and because Crescent City, in northern California, had been struck by a deadly tsunami triggered by the March 1964 Alaska earthquake. Similarly, when

Hurricane Rita struck Texas and western Louisiana in 2005, officials were quick to evacuate Galveston and other low-lying areas, in large part because the poor preparation for Hurricane Katrina was fresh in their minds.

I have sought in this study to understand whether and to what extent earthquakes and hurricanes in one place influenced policy-making elsewhere. The answer is mixed at best. It appears that states that suffer a disaster are more likely to learn from that disaster than are states that do not directly experience the disaster. To the extent that learning does take place, it may be more a function of the accumulation of knowledge rather than from a single event. Future research should address the question of how one would empirically measure the accumulation of experience and its role in policy learning.

Policy Implementation and Lessons

This study does not consider the extent to which "lessons," in the form of policy changes, are actually put into practice. At least three outcomes can follow event-related policy change. The first occurs when the policy change improves policy performance by preventing or mitigating future events, thereby positively reinforcing the policy. Disasters serve as both a feedback mechanism and a reminder to policymakers of the importance of continued efforts to make good policy. The second outcome occurs when policy change fails to improve performance or creates even worse outcomes than the previous policy. This is the situation we face today with much of the current policy on natural disasters, which emphasizes relief and recovery rather than mitigation. This emphasis actually encourages people to build in flood-prone areas and otherwise behave in ways they wouldn't if government policies did not distort their sense of self-interest by shifting the risk from individuals to society as a whole. The third outcome occurs when policy change has no impact because it is hampered by the usual dynamics of multiple levels of government and chains of command, communication breakdowns, or the resistance of local officials or target populations.

The research outlined in this book could thus be extended to consider what we might call event-related policy implementation. This type of policy implementation might work in two ways. In one case we would see the implementation of a new policy triggered by an event—for example, the creation of the Transportation Security Administration, a clear outgrowth of the September 11 attacks. In another case we would see a renewed effort to implement an existing policy that had been inadequately enforced—for example, increased vigilance by airport security officials in passenger screening. Experience shows that this kind of increased vigilance will decay over time as memories of the triggering event fade and as events in other policy domains have spillover effects. In both cases cumulative experience is important to shaping implementation processes and outcomes. It may take multiple attempts before policy change is achieved.

Hurricane Katrina and the Unlearning of Lessons

The predominant question posed in media coverage after Hurricane Katrina devastated New Orleans was, "How could the response have been so poor?" This question also dominated a special congressional hearing at which FEMA director Michael Brown was roundly castigated by the predominantly Republican panel for his apparently fumbling response to the disaster.

Even if New Orleans had weathered the "usual" large hurricane, this storm would have received a great deal of attention in at least three states. The damage to the Alabama and Mississippi gulf coasts was astonishing. The mayor of Biloxi called Katrina "our tsunami," a claim that might have seemed exaggerated at first but that was borne out by the extent of the devastation. Boats, cars, houses, and debris were driven hundreds of yards inland by a storm surge wave estimated as high as thirty feet. Pictures of Biloxi looked very much like those of Thailand and Sri Lanka after the 2004 tsunami.

The main story, however, focused on the inundation in New Orleans. Levees failed in large part because of engineering and construction flaws, flooding nearly 80 percent of the city and displacing several hundred thousand citizens. It appears that many of these people will be displaced for a long time, if not permanently; as of early 2006 approximately half of the displaced have not returned to New Orleans, and many of them have started new lives elsewhere. The damage done to New Orleans by Hurricane Katrina is consistent with scenarios that had been anticipated and studied by journalists, academics, and professional emergency managers for years. There was a widespread conviction among these professionals that the catastrophic flooding of the city was a matter of when, not if, unless serious measures were taken to shore up levees, upgrade pumps, and adequately plan for the evacuation of all citizens of New Orleans, not just those who had cars or could afford plane tickets.

Even given the failure to plan and prepare for a storm like Katrina, the story might have been different had the federal, state and local response to the storm not been so inept. FEMA director Michael Brown's apparent incompetence and mismanagement have been well documented, and he was dismissed from the post as a result. Although Brown's defense, in congressional hearings and the media, did little to inspire confidence in his leadership, Brown was correct about at least one thing: The federal emergency preparedness and management system is intended to support, not supplant, state and local efforts. Of course, the federal dimension of hurricane management was designed in the first place for precisely the sort of catastrophe that Katrina turned out to be: an event that entirely overwhelmed the state and local emergency management system.

How is it that the federal government's response to Katrina could be so poor, when responses to natural disasters in the 1990s were generally viewed as competent? Clearly, the size of Katrina is part of the answer. This was no mere disaster: Rather, it was a catastrophe that overwhelmed local and state governments (Quarantelli 2005). Yet a similar event occurred in 1992 when Hurricane Andrew struck Florida. The following passage describes the reaction to Hurricane Andrew and its impact on FEMA's credibility and support in Congress.

> [FEMA's] state of decline and lack of credibility eventually reached a crisis point during Hurricane Andrew in 1992. The decision by the Bush Administration to turn to the secretary of transportation as a special presidential representative to head up relief efforts and

to massively involve the armed forces only emphasized the total lack of confidence in FEMA's capabilities.

In the wake of disaster, there were calls from Congress to either abolish the agency, to turn the emergency management over to the military, or to disperse elements of the program to other organizations with both the federal and state levels of government. (Schroeder, Wamsley, and Ward 2001, 362)

One could substitute "Katrina" for "Andrew" and "a Coast Guard admiral" for "the secretary of transportation." Indeed, Andrew and Katrina bookend an important story of both the potential for policy learning and the possibility of unlearning lessons when "bigger" problems intrude on mass and elite consciousness.

The 1993 flooding of the Midwest was among the most catastrophic flooding in American history. Yet James Lee Witt's FEMA was widely praised for its relatively effective response and its support of state and local response. Witt, a disaster professional—unlike Michael Brown, a political appointee with no experience in managing disasters—knew that FEMA required significant reform when he took the helm, and he was assured by the Clinton administration that he could appoint his own people without undue interference from the White House. FEMA under Witt was not to be the "turkey farm" it had been under the inept administration of its previous directors, most of whom were political appointees rather than professionals (Tierney 2005).

When the Bush administration took over in 2001, it returned to the political model of FEMA appointments. Bush first appointed Joe Allbaugh, his aide and campaign manager from Texas and a member of his "iron triangle" of advisors, to head FEMA (Michael Brown was appointed FEMA general counsel and later replaced Allbaugh as FEMA's director). Very early in his tenure Allbaugh revealed his ignorance of current trends in flood mitigation, castigating Davenport, Iowa, for not building a floodwall. As it turned out, the city had removed a considerable number of buildings from the floodplain rather than build a floodwall, and in this way avoided the mistakes that other communities had made in allowing development right up to the floodwall. This and other early troubling signs—the termination of Project Impact and funding cuts for the HMGP—revealed the retrograde direction of disaster policy at FEMA under the Bush administration.

Even so, one wonders whether the response to Katrina would have been so poor had FEMA not been merged into the DHS. With the September 11 attacks and the creation of the DHS, the management of emergencies became extremely salient in American politics, and this was amplified even further by the mysterious and frightening anthrax attacks in October 2001. The popular consensus at the time was that the emergency response system needed to be substantially revamped. Lost in much of this discussion was the fact that, in terms of response to the September 11 attacks, the system worked reasonably well. Tragic losses certainly occurred in the course of the response; the death of more than 350 fire fighters, police officers, and other rescuers might have been avoided had command and communications systems been more robust. Even so, and even with the loss of the Emergency Operations Center (EOC) in 7 WTC, the City of New York, supported (not supplanted) by state and federal resources, was able to improvise quickly and effectively, and within forty-eight hours had established a new, functioning EOC on Pier 92. The emergency management system in place on September 11 was not perfect, and every event provides opportunities for learning and improvement, but it functioned reasonably well.

As the 9/11 Commission found, the September 11 attacks resulted primarily from a "failure of imagination." The agencies and officials responsible for collecting and analyzing intelligence and law enforcement information failed to imagine the possibility that terrorists would hijack planes and crash them into buildings. In the wake of the attacks we learned that the FBI and CIA had not shared information effectively and that it was even difficult for information from FBI field offices to be channeled to higher levels where it could be correlated with other information and patterns could be discerned. In short, one can make a strong case that the September 11 attacks revealed not an emergency management problem but problems in intelligence, law enforcement, and national security that existing institutions were unable to address effectively.

Still, emergency management was swept up into the bigger issue of "homeland security" because, as Kathleen Tierney notes, September 11 made the issue so big that nearly everyone wanted a piece of the action:

Whereas disasters had always been very low on local, state, and federal policy agendas, terrorism was important—by which I mean that for the first time, serious money was available to help make our society safer in the face of extreme events. A volatile mix of outrage, patriotism, politics, the profit motive, and entrenched institutional interests reshaped not only agencies and programs, but perhaps more important, the overall strategy this society would use in its preparations for future threats of all types. The emerging homeland security complex provided almost unlimited opportunities for both the private sector and for government agencies. (Tierney 2005)

The participants in this homeland security boom did not let their ignorance of disaster policy or of individual and community behavior in disasters stop them from proposing ideas that were sometimes uninformed and relatively innocuous but sometimes dangerous. The color-coded "threat advisory system" was unhelpful but probably not dangerous compared with the wholesale gutting of FEMA, the rejection of its more successful programs relating to hazard mitigation, and the burying of the agency in a new department dominated by intelligence, law enforcement, and military officials.

Tierney continues:

New DHS programs placed little emphasis on improving preparedness and response programs for any emergencies, including both terrorist attacks and disasters. Instead, the overwhelming emphasis was on detection, prevention, and deterrence of terrorist attacks. . . . New DHS policies and programs violated two fundamental principles of emergency management. First, both social science research and emergency management practice have long emphasized the value of using an "all hazards" approach . . . meaning that communities and other governmental levels should assess their vulnerabilities, focus generically on tasks that must be performed regardless of event type, and then plan for specific contingencies, guided by risk-based assessments of what could happen. Despite the fact that DHS claims to approach emergency management from an "all hazards" and risk-based perspective, concerns related to terrorism and weapons of mass destruction dominate agency programs. . . . Second, since the late 1970s, emergency management research and practice have emphasized what is termed "comprehensive emergency management," or the notion that loss-reduction efforts should be carried out in an integrated way across different time phases of extreme events. . . . Yet DHS has created stovepipes that work against such integration. Within DHS, the concept of mitigation has all but disappeared—except, of course, with respect to prevention and deterrence of terrorist attacks—and most emergency preparedness activities are assigned not to FEMA, which retains responsibility for response and recovery, but to other branches within DHS . . . [that] focus almost exclusively on funding and providing guidance for terrorism-related preparedness programs across the U.S.

This lengthy passage substantiates my point: FEMA's traditional functions were hollowed out, its most experienced staff have left the agency, morale is in shambles, and the agency in which it is embedded, the DHS, is far less concerned with an "all-hazards" approach than it is with terrorism.

What can policy process theory and my theory of event-related policy learning tell us about what has happened in emergency management since September 11, 2001? A particularly apt explanation is provided by John Kingdon (1995), who notes that the behavior of the different "streams" of the policy process is influenced by "spillovers" from other policy domains. In this case, as Tierney notes, the homeland security domain is so large, the issues it addresses so important, and its organization so dominant that what happened is more a tsunami than a spillover. FEMA was entirely overwhelmed by the new homeland security imperative, and even if it had remained a separate agency, we cannot know (though there is little reason to believe) that FEMA's efforts in disaster mitigation would have received as much attention during the Bush administration, particularly after September 11, as they did during the Clinton years.

Indeed, September 11 turned the disaster field on its head. Most practitioners and academic experts believed that the all-hazards approach advanced at FEMA under James Lee Witt could be extended to terrorism—as indeed it was at the outset of the first Bush administration. But the homeland security establishment that sprang up after September 11 assumed that all disasters looked like terrorism and that FEMA could be redirected to focus on responding to terrorism while continuing the old, less exciting work of dealing with natural disasters.

The shift of FEMA's emphasis to response to terrorist attacks should not be overstated. The agency continues to support state and local responses to natural disasters, and during the 2004 hurricane season its performance was viewed as relatively good. FEMA did, however, respond to a series of storms that, even in the aggregate, were far lest catastrophic than Hurricane Katrina, and a series of storms that primarily struck Florida, which had learned from Hurricane Andrew and had taken effective steps to prepare for, respond to, and mitigate natural disasters. This was not the case in Louisiana, which was demonstrably unprepared for a storm of the size and scale of Katrina, regardless of FEMA's failures. But FEMA is now primarily responsible for relief, its role in hazard mitigation is greatly diminished, and it is fair to say that much of what was learned and implemented as policy in the 1990s has been undone under the Bush administration.

We can see, then, evidence of two kinds of "unlearning." The first happens when lessons simply decay over time. The second occurs when a lesson is overtaken by an event that triggers policies that undermine the original lesson. Bush's decision to appoint political cronies with no experience in disaster management to top posts at FEMA, coupled with his administration's shift away from mitigation efforts, weakened the agency substantially. The September 11 attacks and FEMA's absorption into the DHS further undermined the agency's effectiveness, to the point that its bungled response to Katrina became as big a story as the disaster itself.

FEMA's many failures in mitigation, preparedness, and response have led to wide-ranging calls that we "learn the lessons" of Katrina. Some of the ideas being discussed suggest that it is possible for people and organizations to learn the wrong lessons— that is, to enact policies that are unlikely to mitigate the negative effects of future events or even make them worse. In the aftermath of Hurricane Katrina, for example, public officials vowed to rebuild New Orleans just as it was before. This is often precisely what happens after a hurricane, and the result is a replication of the very vulnerabilities that made the damage so bad in the first place. Defining the "right" and "wrong" lessons from a disaster like Katrina is beyond the scope of this book, in part because this is a deeply normative question and in part because my goal here is to understand how policy change is triggered by events. Additional research could certainly develop a set of criteria for what the lessons of a given event *should* be, and could then assess whether those lessons are learned and are applied to better policy. Time will tell whether the "lessons" of Katrina being bandied about in the popular and technical media and in federal, state, and local governments are actually learned and translated into policy, or are simply observed and filed away until the next disaster causes policymakers and reporters to rediscover these original "lessons."

This book, like any in the social sciences, is hardly the last word on policy change related to events. Sophisticated analytic techniques can be employed to discover why policies change at particular times and particular places. Nevertheless, this study has revealed important features about event-related policymaking that suggest that policies are the product of learning from disasters. Learning from disasters is, in the end, something citizens expect government to do. People believe strongly that governments, companies, and organizations, just like people themselves, should learn from their mistakes. While actual learning is often confounded by other expectations that the public has of policymakers and institutions, evidence suggests that when a problem is sufficiently serious to gain widespread attention, learning and improved policy will follow. When learning does happen—when policy does improve because new information is acted upon—it is important to recognize this learning when it happens, to show how it is possible, and to encourage continuous policy learning and improvement wherever possible.

notes

Chapter 1

1. My definition of a focusing event is narrower than Kingdon's; his definition includes events that can happen to individual members of a policy community that influence their attitudes toward policy. For example, some members of Congress become interested in particular diseases when they or members of their families become afflicted (Kingdon 1995, 94–95).

2. This quotation is available in various sources. I found it at "American Experience: The Presidents: Franklin D. Roosevelt," http://www.pbs.org/wgbh/amex/presidents/32_f_roosevelt/tguide/f_roosevelt_iq.html (accessed June 20, 2005). A more systematic approach of experimentation and policy adaptation is outlined in Holling (1978).

3. A standard treatment of the idea of policy tools generally is found in Salamon and Elliott (2002).

4. One such fatal cockpit intrusion took place in 1987, when Pacific Southwest Airlines Flight 1771 crashed after a disgruntled former employee of another airline used his employee credentials to bypass security with a gun, board a plane carrying his supervisor, and shoot the supervisor, the flight crew, and then himself. The plane, its pilots dead, plunged to earth, killing all forty-three persons aboard. This incident was ultimately seen as a failure of security to screen individuals with airline

credentials, not as a failure of cockpit security, and incremental changes were made to security procedures at airports. In particular, flight crew members were to be screened at checkpoints along with passengers. The accident report is available from the National Transportation Safety Board, www.ntsb.gov.

5. "[O]ften a front-page story in that morning's *Times* appears near the top of a newscast. 'It's in your own city, so it's easy,' said Susan Zirinsky, a CBS executive producer, who thinks that such shortcuts too often replace 'enterprise reporting.' Andy Rooney, who joined CBS as a writer forty-four years ago, and who has also been a news producer, says, 'It's infuriating. If it wasn't for the *New York Times*, network news would have to shut down'" (Auletta 2005).

Chapter 2

1. On this point, see "What Is Terrorism?" at "September 11 Attacks: Background and Aftermath," http://www.askasia.org/teachers/Instructional_Resources/FEATURES/AmericasCrisis/BG1/whatisterrorism.htm (accessed June 16, 2005).

2. The timeline is available as a large PDF file at http://www.disaster-timeline.com/ttl.html.

3. This shift in thinking signals an important change in the way we think about how to prepare for potential disasters. Lee Clarke pioneered this shift in an article in *Natural Hazards Observer* (2005a), and he has expanded his argument in a new book titled *Worst Cases: Terror and Catastrophe in the Popular Imagination* (2005b).

4. I acknowledge that the October 2001 anthrax mailings were also important and that they further fueled discussions of the terrorist threat to the United States, but I focus primarily on outcomes from the September 11 attacks, which, I argue, had a much more profound influence on agenda and policy change.

5. Because I am seeking to establish the September 11 attacks as a key national issue rather than merely as a question of foreign policy, I focus only on the national, metro, and foreign desks here. I also collected data on the editorial desk, which are omitted from this figure both for purposes of clarity and because the numbers track very closely with the national agenda. I also calculated these data for the sports, arts and leisure, financial, and Sunday Week in Review desks. These data track very closely with the national desk index, except for the finance desk, which had an index score of 7686 for 2001, reflecting the

great importance of the WTC and the affected area to world and national financial markets.

6. Jay Rockefeller, *Congressional Record,* 107th Cong., 2d sess. (October 4, 2001): S. 10270.

7. Unless otherwise noted, all polling data in this book are found on the "Polling the Nations" database available at many academic libraries. Information is available at http://www.orspub.com/.

Chapter 3

1. For summaries of these incidents, see Rubin et al. (2003). For a reasonably balanced journalistic account of the TWA 800 accident, see Negroni (2000).

2. Examples of this literature include popular exposés. A pre–September 11 example is Mary Schiavo's *Flying Blind, Flying Safe* (1997), in which the former inspector general of the Department of Transportation issued a blistering indictment of the safety and security record of the aviation industry. Security is more explicitly considered in a sometimes breathless post–September 11 book by Andrew Thomas, *Aviation Insecurity: The New Challenges of Air Travel* (2003), in which the author notes the numerous failings of aviation security— many of them detailed here—before the September 11 hijackings, and concludes that the post–September 11 measures are unlikely to do much to deter a determined terrorist in a future attack. The aviation trade press tends be much more technical, oriented toward day-to-day operations, and unsurprisingly pro-industry for the most part. There is a relatively small body of political science or public policy literature on aviation safety and security. The best recent example, on which much of this analysis relies, is *The Plane Truth: Airline Crashes, the Media, and Transportation Policy* (Cobb and Primo 2003), a study of the interaction between aviation accidents and attacks, the news media, and the regulatory system.

3. While many airport operators are public or quasi public agencies, I categorize these organizations as private-sector organizations because their interests are more clearly aligned with the aviation sector than with government regulators.

4. In 2004 the General Accounting Office changed its name to the Government Accountability Office to reflect the fact that the bulk of GAO's work is not financial accounting and auditing. See http://www.gao.gov/about/namechange.html.

Chapter 4

1. The U.S. Geological Survey explains the moment magnitude scale as follows: "Moment is a physical quantity proportional to the slip on the fault times the area of the fault surface that slips; it is related to the total energy released in the earthquake. The moment can be estimated from seismograms (and also from geodetic measurements). The moment is then converted into a number similar to other earthquake magnitudes by a standard formula. The result is called the moment magnitude. The moment magnitude provides an estimate of earthquake size that is valid over the complete range of magnitudes, a characteristic that was lacking in other magnitude scales." This means that moment magnitude provides a more accurate measure of the energy released by the largest earthquakes than the Richter scale does. See the Geological Survey's "Frequently Asked Questions" site at http://earthquake.usgs.gov/faq/meas.html. For the equation for deriving the moment magnitude of an earthquake, see http://en.wikipedia.org/wiki/Moment_magnitude_scale. The equation is scaled in a way that makes the moment magnitude close, but not equal, to Richter magnitude figures.

2. For the entire scale, see the website on the modified Mercalli intensity scale maintained by the Association of Bay Area Governments at http://www.abag.ca.gov/bayarea/eqmaps/doc/mmi.html.

3. My preference would have been to code the *Los Angeles Times* and the *Miami Herald* as the key papers for earthquakes and hurricanes, respectively, but LexisNexis does not contain the full text of these papers for the time spans in question. However, there is little in the literature to suggest that the coverage of disasters by these large papers differs substantially from the papers I ultimately used. I also sought to collect data on the Loma Prieta earthquake, but the LexisNexis databases I used do not go back to 1989. And the *Raleigh News and Observer* is available on Lexis-Nexis only to 1996, which did not allow me to analyze stories on Hurricane Andrew.

4. See the letter by Janet Meshek at the Association of State Floodplain Managers website, http://www.floods.org/policy/OK_Position_Paper.pdf.

5. For Washington State's earthquake program, see http://emd.wa.gov/3-map/mit/eq-tsunami/eq-idx.htm. The website address of the California Seismic Safety Commission is http://www.seismic.ca.gov/.

6. On the general issue of industry opposition to more stringent mitigation measures, see Prater and Lindell (2000).

7. See North Carolina Disaster Recovery Task Force at http://www.dem.dcc.state.nc.us/taskforce/execsum.htm, and its table of

actions taken at http://www.dem.dcc.state.nc.us/taskforce/taskforce2.htm (both accessed May 20, 2006).

Chapter 5

1. It is difficult to do a similar search on particular earthquakes, because earthquakes are not widely known by a single name. Names like the Loma Prieta and Northridge earthquakes tend to be well known to technical experts, but there are numerous variations, including the San Francisco or World Series earthquake and the Los Angeles earthquake.

references

Alberts, Sheldon. 2004. "We are not safe," Americans told: Dramatic reforms urged to prevent next 9/11. *Ottawa Citizen,* July 23, A6.

Alesch, Daniel J., and William J. Petak. 1986. *Politics and economics of earthquake hazard mitigation: Unreinforced masonry buildings in Southern California.* Boulder: University of Colorado, Natural Hazards Research and Applications Information Center.

———. 2001. *Overcoming obstacles to implementation: Addressing political, institutional, and behavioral problems in earthquake hazard mitigation policies.* Buffalo: Multidisciplinary Center for Earthquake Engineering Research.

Associated Press. 2001. "Davenport awaits river crest." *Dubuque Telegraph Herald,* April 25, C6.

Auletta, Ken. 2005. Sign off. *New Yorker,* September 20, 48–60.

Baker, Earl J. 1993. Coastal development invites hurricane damage. *USA Today Magazine,* May, 68–70.

Baumgartner, Frank R., and Bryan D. Jones. 1993. *Agendas and instability in American politics.* Chicago: University of Chicago Press.

Bennett, Colin J., and Michael Howlett. 1992. The lessons of learning: Reconciling theories of policy learning and policy change. *Policy Sciences* 25 (3): 275–94.

Birkland, Thomas A. 1997a. *After disaster: Agenda setting, public policy, and focusing events.* Washington, DC: Georgetown University Press.

———. 1997b. Factors inhibiting a national hurricane policy. *Coastal Management* 25 (4): 387–403.

———. 1998. Focusing events, mobilization, and agenda setting. *Journal of Public Policy* 18 (3): 53–74.

———. 2001. Our political system will keep doing its job. *Albany Times Union*, September 30, B1.

———. 2004. Learning and policy improvement after disaster: The case of aviation security. *American Behavioral Scientist* 48 (3): 341–64.

Birkland, Thomas A., Raymond J. Burby, David Conrad, Hanna Cortner, and William K. Michener. 2003. River ecology and flood hazard mitigation. *Natural Hazards Review* 4 (1): 46–54.

Birkland, Thomas A., and Radhika Nath. 2000. Business and the political dimension in disaster management. *Journal of Public Policy* 20 (3): 279–303.

Bishop, Sanford, Jr. 2002. Homeland security information sharing act. *Congressional Record*, 107th Cong., 2d sess. (June 26): H 3940.

Bond, David. 2003. No longer needed? Airlines say the FAA fumbled the analysis of benefits, cost, and feasibility for the transponder hijack rule. *Aviation Week and Space Technology* 158 (18): 46.

Booth, S. 1993. *Crisis management strategy: Competition and change in modern enterprises.* New York: Routledge.

Briechle, Kendra J. 1999. Natural hazard mitigation and local government decision making. In *The Municipal Yearbook 1999.* Washington, DC: International City/County Management Association.

Burby, Raymond J. 1994. Floodplain planning and management: Research needed for the 21st century. *Water Resources Update* 97: 44–47.

———. 2005. Have state comprehensive planning mandates reduced insured losses from natural disasters? *Natural Hazards Review* 6 (2): 67–81.

Burby, Raymond J., and Linda C. Dalton. 1993. State planning mandates and coastal management. In *Coastal zone '93,* ed. W. Stanley Wilson, Orville T. Magoon, Hugh Converse, and L. Tomas Tobin, 1069–83. New York: American Society of Civil Engineers.

Burby, Raymond J., Steven P. French, and Arthur C. Nelson. 1998. Plans, code enforcement, and damage reduction: Evidence from the Northridge earthquake. *Earthquake Spectra* 14 (1): 59–74.

Burkholder, JoAnn, David Eggleston, Howard Glasgow, Cavell Brownie, Robert Reed, Gerald Janowitz, Martin Posey, Greg Melia, Carol Kinder, Reide Corbett, David Toms, Troy Alphin, Nora Deamer, and Jeffrey Springer. 2004. Comparative impacts of two major hurricane seasons on the Neuse River and western Pamlico Sound ecosystems. *Proceedings of the National Academy of Sciences* 101 (25): 9291–96.

Burstein, Paul. 1991. Policy domains: Organization, culture, and policy outcomes. *Annual Review of Sociology* 17: 327–50.

Busenberg, George J. 2001. Learning in organizations and public policy. *Journal of Public Policy* 21 (2): 173–89.

California Governor's Office of Emergency Management. 2004. *State of California multi hazard mitigation plan.* Rancho Cordova, CA: Governor's Office of Emergency Management.

Carter, W. N. 1991. *Disaster management: A disaster manager's handbook.* Manila: Asian Development Bank.

Clarke, Lee. 2003. Introduction: 9/11 as disaster; on worst cases, terrorism, and catastrophe. *Research in Social Problems and Public Policy* 11: 1–6.

———. 2005a. Worst-case thinking: An idea whose time has come. *Natural Hazards Observer* 29 (3): 1–3.

———. 2005b. *Worst cases: Terror and catastrophe in the popular imagination.* Chicago: University of Chicago Press.

Cobb, Roger W., and David M. Primo. 2003. *The plane truth: Airline crashes, the media, and transportation policy.* Washington, DC: Brookings Institution.

Cobb, Roger, Jeannie-Keith Ross, and Marc Howard Ross. 1976. Agenda building as a comparative political process. *American Political Science Review* 70 (1): 126–38.

Cochrane, H., J. E. Haas, D. J. Amaral, R. A. Olson, and M. Bowden. 1974. *Social science perspectives on the coming San Francisco earthquake— Economic impact, prediction, and reconstruction.* Working Paper 25. Boulder: University of Colorado, Natural Hazards Research and Applications Information Center.

Conrad, David, Martha Stout, and Ben McNitt. 1998. *Higher ground: A report on voluntary property buyouts in the nation's floodplains.* Vienna, VA: National Wildlife Federation.

Crowley, Walt. 2003. *Challengers Mark Sidran and Greg Nickels outpoll incumbent Mayor Paul Schell in primary election on September 18, 2001.* http://www.historylink.org/essays/output.cfm?file_id=3663 (accessed December 3, 2005).

Dalton, Linda C., and Raymond J. Burby. 1994. Mandates, plans and planners: Building local commitment to development management. *Journal of the American Planning Association* 60 (autumn): 444–61.

Darton, Eric. 1999. *Divided we stand: A biography of New York's World Trade Center.* New York: Basic Books.

Davidson, Roger H., and Walter J. Oleszek. 1994. *Congress and its members.* Washington, DC: Congressional Quarterly Press.

Doig, Jameson W. 2001. *Empire on the Hudson: Entrepreneurial vision and political power at the Port of New York Authority.* New York: Columbia University Press.

Downs, Anthony. 1972. Up and down with ecology: The issue attention cycle. *Public Interest* 28 (summer): 38–50.

Dunkelberger, Lloyd. 2005. Building code sparks debate; hurricane-prone counties may need higher standards for wind protection; Panhandle exemption. *Lakeland (Fla.) Ledger,* August 8, B1.

Dye, Thomas R. 1992. *Understanding public policy.* 7th ed. Englewood Cliffs, NJ: Prentice Hall.

Etheredge, Lloyd S. 1985. *Can governments learn? American foreign policy and Central American revolutions.* New York: Pergamon Press.

Faulkner, Bill. 2001. Towards a framework for tourism disaster management. *Tourism Management* 22: 135–41.

Federal Emergency Management Agency (FEMA). 1992. *Building for the future: National earthquake hazards reduction program, fiscal years 1991–1992 report to Congress.* Washington, DC: Federal Emergency Management Agency.

Fenlon, Brodie, and Philip Lee-Shanock. 2001. Hellfire down on their heads. *Toronto Sun,* September 11, 9.

Florida Department of Community Affairs. 1995. Summary of state and local emergency management capabilities. Tallahassee: Florida Department of Community Affairs.

Geschwind, Carl-Henry. 2001. *California earthquakes: Science, risk, and the politics of hazard mitigation.* Baltimore: Johns Hopkins University Press.

Gillespie, Angus K. 2002. *Twin towers: The life of New York City's World Trade Center.* Rev. ed. New York: New American Library.

Godschalk, David, Timothy Beatley, Philip Berke, David J. Brower, and Edward J. Kaiser. 1998. *Natural hazard mitigation.* Washington, DC: Island Press.

Goggin, Malcolm L., James Lester, Lawrence O'Toole, and Ann Bowman. 1990. *Implementation theory and practice: Toward a third generation.* Glenview, IL: Scott, Foresman and Co.

Governor's Disaster Planning and Response Review Committee. 1993. *Report of the governor's disaster planning and response review committee.* Tallahassee: State of Florida, Governor's Disaster Planning and Response Review Committee.

Greenhouse, Linda M. 2002. Executive decisions: A penchant for secrecy. *New York Times,* May 3, sec. 4, p. 1.

Grossback, Lawrence J., Sean Nicholson-Crotty, and David A. M. Patterson. 2004. Ideology and learning in policy diffusion. *American Politics Research* 32 (5): 521–45.

Hall, Peter A. 1988. Policy paradigms, social learning, and the state. Paper presented at a meeting of the International Political Science Association, Washington, DC.

———. 1993. Policy paradigms, social learning, and the state: The case of economic policymaking in Britain. *Comparative Politics* 25: 275–96.

Harte, John. 2001. Land use, biodiversity, and ecosystem integrity: The challenge of preserving earth's life support system. *Ecology Law Quarterly* 27 (4): 929–66.

Heclo, Hugh. 1974. *Modern social policies in Britain and Sweden.* New Haven: Yale University Press.

Hilgartner, James, and Charles Bosk. 1988. The rise and fall of social problems: A public arenas model. *American Journal of Sociology* 94 (1): 53–78.

Holling, C. S. 1978. *Adaptive environmental assessment and management.* Chichester, NY: Wiley.

ISO Properties. 2005. What? Why? When? And what do I do? http://www.isomitigation.com/bcegs/0000/bcegs0002.html (accessed June 10, 2005).

Jones, Bryan D. 2001. *Politics and the architecture of choice: Bounded rationality and governance.* Chicago: University of Chicago Press.

Kingdon, John W. 1995. *Agendas, alternatives, and public policies.* 2d ed. New York: Harper Collins.

Knoke, David, and Edward O. Laumann. 1982. The social organization of national policy domains: An exploration of some structural hypotheses. In *Social structure and network analysis,* ed. Peter V. Marsden and Nan Lin, 255–70. Beverly Hills, CA: Sage Publications.

Kreps, Gary A. 1990. The federal emergency management system in the United States: Past and present. *International Journal of Mass Emergencies and Disasters* 8 (3): 275–300.

Langer, Gary. 2002. Six months later: Poll finds support for Bush, war on terrorism isn't fading. http://abcnews.go.com/sections/us/DailyNews/poll_sixmonths020311.html.

Laumann, Edward O., and David Knoke. 1987. *The organizational state: Social choice in national policy domains.* Madison: University of Wisconsin Press.

Lawrence, Regina G. 2000a. Game-framing the news: Tracking the strategy frame in public policy news. *Political Communication* 17: 93–114.

———. 2000b. *The politics of force: Media and the construction of police brutality.* Berkeley and Los Angeles: University of California Press.

Lawrence, Regina G., and Thomas A. Birkland. 2004. Guns, Hollywood, and criminal justice: Defining the school shootings problem across public arenas. *Social Science Quarterly* 85 (5): 1193–1207.

Leahy, Patrick. 2001. Combating international terrorism. *Congressional Record*, 107th Cong., 1st sess. (November 1): S 11356–59.

Learmount, David. 2003. Hijack transponder "no longer needed"; pilots may be reluctant to use emergency code, says AEA. *Flight International*, March 4, 5.

Levy, J. 1994. Learning and foreign policy: Sweeping a conceptual minefield. *International Organization* 48 (2): 279–312.

Lipsky, Michael. 1978. Toward a theory of street-level bureaucracy. *Urban Affairs Quarterly* 6 (June): 391–409.

Lowi, Theodore. 1964. American business, public policy, case studies, and political theory. *World Politics* 16: 677–93.

May, Peter J. 1985. *Recovering from catastrophes: Federal disaster relief policy and politics.* Westport, CT: Greenwood Press.

———. 1990. Reconsidering policy design: Policies and publics. *Journal of Public Policy* 11 (2): 187–206.

———. 1992. Policy learning and failure. *Journal of Public Policy* 12 (4): 331–54.

———. 1993. Mandate design and implementation: Enhancing implementation efforts and shaping regulatory styles. *Journal of Policy Analysis and Management* 10 (2): 634–63.

May, Peter J., and Thomas A. Birkland. 1994. Earthquake risk reduction: An examination of local regulatory efforts. *Environmental Management* 18 (6): 923–39.

May, Peter J., Edward Fox, and Nancy Stark Hasan. 1989. *Anticipating earthquakes: Risk reduction policies and practices in the Puget Sound and Portland areas.* Seattle: University of Washington, Graduate School of Public Affairs, Institute for Public Policy and Management.

McInnis, Scott. 2001. Providing safety in the skies. *Congressional Record*, 107th Cong., 1st sess. (October 16): H 6898–900.

Mead, Kenneth. 2002. "Challenges Facing TSA in Implementing the Aviation and Transportation Security Act." Statement before the U.S. House of Representatives, Committee on Transportation and Infrastructure, Subcommittee on Aviation, January 23. http://www.house.gov/transportation/aviation/01-23-02/mead.html (accessed May 20, 2006).

Merari, Ariel. 1999. Attacks on civil aviation: Trends and lessons. In *Aviation terrorism and security,* ed. Paul Wilkinson and Brian Michael Jenkins, 9–26. London: Frank Cass.

Millender-McDonald, Juanita. 2001. Historic compromise on aviation security. *Congressional Record*, 107th Cong., 1st sess. (November 15): H 8231.

Miller, George. 2002. Independent commission needs to determine facts. *Congressional Record*, 107th Cong., 2d sess. (May 22): H 2926.

Mittler, Elliott. 1997. *A case study of Florida's emergency management since Hurricane Andrew*. Working Paper 98. Boulder: University of Colorado, Natural Hazards Research and Applications Information Center. http://www.colorado.edu/hazards/wp/wp98.html (accessed May 20, 2006).

———. 1998. *A case study of the enactment of a state building code in South Carolina*. Working Paper 96. Boulder: University of Colorado, Natural Hazards Research and Applications Information Center. http://www.colorado.edu/hazards/wp/wp96.html.

Molotch, Harvey. 1970. Santa Barbara: Oil in the velvet playground. In *Eco-Catastrophe*, 84–105. New York: Harper and Row.

Multihazard Mitigation Council, National Institute of Building Sciences. 2005. *Natural hazard mitigation saves: An independent study to assess the future savings from mitigation activities*. Vol. 1, *Findings, conclusions, and recommendations*. Washington, DC: National Institute of Building Sciences.

National Academy of Sciences, Committee on the Alaska Earthquake of the Division of Earth Sciences, National Research Council. 1973. *The great Alaska earthquake of 1964: Summary and recommendations*. Washington, DC: National Academy of Sciences.

National Commission on Terrorist Attacks upon the United States (9/11 Commission). 2004. *The 9/11 Commission report: Final report of the National Commission on Terrorist Attacks upon the United States*. Authorized ed. New York: W. W. Norton.

National Research Council, Commission on Geosciences, Environment, and Resources, U.S. National Committee for the Decade for Natural Disaster Reduction. 1991. *A safer future: Reducing the impacts of natural disasters*. Washington, DC: National Academy Press.

Negroni, Christine. 2000. *Deadly departure: Why the experts failed to prevent the TWA Flight 800 disaster and how it could happen again*. New York: Cliff Street/HarperCollins.

Nice, David C., and Ashley Grosse. 2001. Crisis policy making: Some implications for program management. In *Handbook of Crisis and Emergency Management*, ed. Ali Farazmand, 55–67. New York: Marcel Dekker.

North Carolina Center for Public Policy Research. 2001. *Center says state must act to prevent future hurricane damage*. http://www.nccppr.org/easternnc1.htm (accessed May 15, 2005).

North Carolina Division of Emergency Management. 2004. *State 322 natural hazard mitigation plan.* Raleigh: North Carolina Division of Emergency Management.

Olson, Mancur. 1971. *The logic of collective action*. Cambridge: Harvard University Press.

Olson, Robert A. 2003. Legislative politics and seismic safety: California's early years and the "Field Act," 1925–1933. *Earthquake Spectra* 19 (1): 111–31.

Ostrom, Elinor. 1999. Institutional rational choice: An assessment of the institutional analysis and development framework. In *Theories of the Policy Process*, ed. Paul A. Sabatier, 35–74. Boulder, CO: Westview Press.

Paerl, Hans W., Jerad D. Bales, Larry W. Ausley, Christopher P. Buzzelli, Larry B. Crowder, Lisa A. Eby, John M. Fear, Malia Go, Benjamin L. Peierls, Tammi L. Richardson, and Joseph S. Ramus. 2001. Ecosystem impacts of three sequential hurricanes (Dennis, Floyd, and Irene) on the United States' largest lagoonal estuary, Pamlico Sound, NC. *Proceedings of the National Academy of Sciences* 98 (10): 5655–60.

Platt, Rutherford H. 1999. *Disasters and democracy*. Washington, DC: Island Press.

Prater, Carla S., and Michael K. Lindell. 2000. Politics of hazard mitigation. *Natural Hazards Review* 1 (2): 73–82.

Quarantelli, E. L. 2005. *Catastrophes are different from disasters: Some implications for crisis planning and managing drawn from Katrina.* Social Science Research Council. http://understandingkatrina.ssrc.org/ Quarantelli (accessed October 21, 2005).

Raines, Howell. 2004. My times. *Atlantic Monthly*, May, 49–71.

Ramsey, James. 2005. The post 9/11 transponder. *Aviation Today*, June 17. http://www.aviationtoday.com/cgi/av/show_mag.cgi?pub=av&mon=0602&file=0602transponders.htm (accessed June 17, 2005).

Regulatory Intelligence Data. 1999. North Carolina, FEMA announce buyout strategy. Industry Group 99, October 14. http://www.elibrary.com (accessed March 11, 2000).

Ripley, Randall, and Grace Franklin. 1984. *Congress, the bureaucracy, and public policy*. 3d ed. Homewood, IL: Dorsey Press.

Robertson, David B., and Dennis R. Judd. 1989. *The development of American public policy: The structure of policy restraint*. Glenview, IL: Scott, Foresman and Co.

Robson, John. 2001. The world changes in Manhattan. *Ottawa Citizen*, September 12, A9.

Rogers, Everett M. 1995. *Diffusion of innovations*. 4th ed. New York: Free Press.

Rose, Richard. 1993. *Lesson-drawing in public policy: A guide to learning across time and space.* Chatham, NJ: Chatham House.

Rosen, Jay. 2002. September 11 in the mind of American journalism. In *Journalism after September 11,* ed. Stuart Allan Barbie Zelizer, 27–35. New York: Routledge.

Rossi, Peter H., James D. Wright, and Eleanor Weber-Burdin. 1982. *Natural hazards and public choice: The state and local politics of hazard mitigation.* New York: Academic Press.

Rubin, Claire B., William B. Cumming, Irmak R. Tanali, and Thomas A. Birkland. 2003. Major terrorism events and their U.S. outcomes (1988–2001). Boulder: University of Colorado, Natural Hazards Research and Applications Information Center. http:// www.colorado.edu/hazards/wp/wp107/wp107.html.

Sabatier, Paul. 1987. Knowledge, policy-oriented learning, and policy change. *Knowledge: Creation, Diffusion, Utilization* 8 (4): 649–92.

———. 1988. An advocacy coalition framework of policy change and the role of policy-oriented learning therein. *Policy Sciences* 21: 129–68.

———. 1991. Toward better theories of the policy process. *PS: Political Science and Politics* 24 (2): 144–56.

———. 1993. Policy change over a decade or more. In *Policy change and learning: An advocacy coalition approach, theoretical lenses on public policy,* ed. Paul A. Sabatier and Hank C. Jenkins-Smith, 13–39. Boulder, CO: Westview Press.

Sabatier, Paul A., and Hank C. Jenkins-Smith, eds. 1993. *Policy change and learning: An advocacy coalition approach, theoretical lenses on public policy.* Boulder, CO: Westview Press.

Salamon, Lester M., and Odus V. Elliott. 2002. *The tools of government: A guide to the new governance.* Oxford: Oxford University Press.

Schiavo, Mary. 1997. *Flying blind, flying safe.* New York: Avon Books.

Schroeder, Aaron, Gary Wamsley, and Robert Ward. 2001. The evolution of emergency management in America: From a painful past to a promising but uncertain future. In *Handbook of Crisis and Emergency Management,* ed. Ali Farazmand, 357–417. New York: Marcel Dekker.

Simon, Herbert Alexander. 1957. *Administrative behavior: A study of decision-making processes in administrative organization.* 2d ed. New York: Macmillan.

Smith, Conrad. 1992. *Media and apocalypse: News coverage of the Yellowstone forest fires, Exxon Valdez oil spill, and Loma Prieta earthquake.* Westport, CT: Greenwood Press.

Srinivasan, Deepa. 2003. Battling hazards with a brand new tool. *Planning* 69 (2): 10–13.

Stallings, Robert A. 1995. *Promoting risk: Constructing the earthquake threat.* New York: DeGruyter.

Steinberg, Michele, and Raymond J. Burby. 2002. Growing safe. *Planning* 68 (4): 22–23.

Stephenson, Crocker. 2001. The morning after: We have changed. *Milwaukee Journal Sentinel*, September 12, 16A.

St. John, Peter. 1999. The politics of aviation terrorism. In *Aviation terrorism and security*, ed. Paul Wilkinson and Brian Michael Jenkins, 27–49. London: Frank Cass.

Stone, Deborah A. 1989. Causal stories and the formation of policy agendas. *Political Science Quarterly* 104 (2): 281–300.

———. 2002. *Policy paradox: The art of political decision making.* Rev. ed. New York: W. W. Norton.

Swichtenberg, Bill. 2002. Hurricane floods pose risk to environment and health, new research reveals. *Water Engineering and Management* 149 (4): 8.

Thomas, Andrew R. 2003. *Aviation insecurity: The new challenges of air travel.* Amherst, NY: Prometheus Books.

Tierney, Kathleen J. 2000. Executive summary: Disaster-resistant communities initiative: Evaluation of the pilot phase, year 2. Newark: University of Delaware, Disaster Research Center.

———. 2005. The red pill. Social Science Research Council. http://understandingkatrina.ssrc.org/Tierney/ (accessed October 21, 2005).

Tuchman, Gaye. 1978. *Making news: A study in the construction of reality.* New York: Free Press.

U.S. Commission on National Security/21st Century. 1999. *New world coming: American security in the 21st century.* Washington, DC: U.S. Commission on National Security/21st Century. http://www.fas.org/man/docs/nwc/nwc.htm.

———. 2001. *Road map for national security: Imperative for change.* Washington, DC: U.S. Commission on National Security/21st Century. http://govinfo.library.unt.edu/nssg/.

U.S. General Accounting Office (GAO). 1988a. *Aviation security: Corrective actions under way, but better inspection guidance still needed.* Washington, DC: General Accounting Office.

———. 1988b. *Aviation security: Improved controls needed to prevent unauthorized access at key airports; report to the secretary of transportation.* Washington, DC: General Accounting Office.

———. 1997. *Aviation safety and security: Challenges to implementing the recommendations of the White House Commission on Aviation Safety and Security.* Washington, DC: General Accounting Office.

———. 1998. *Aviation security: Implementation of recommendations is under way, but completion will take several years.* Washington, DC: General Accounting Office.

———. 2000a. *Aviation security: Slow progress in addressing long-standing screener performance problems.* Washington, DC: General Accounting Office.

———. 2000b. *Aviation security: Vulnerabilities still exist in the aviation security system.* Washington, DC: General Accounting Office.

———. 2001. *Aviation security: Terrorist acts illustrate severe weaknesses in aviation security.* Washington, DC: General Accounting Office.

University of North Carolina, Office of the President. 2001. *Proposal for the Institute of Disaster Studies.* Chapel Hill: University of North Carolina. http://www.geoearth.uncc.edu/transpol/Disaster/InstituteOfDis Studies10_19.pdf (accessed June 1, 2005).

Washington, State of. Washington Military Department, Emergency Management Division. 2004. *State of Washington hazard mitigation plan.* Olympia: State of Washington.

Weisbecker, Leo W., Ward C. Stoneman, Susan E. Ackerman, Robert K. Arnold, Pamela M. Halton, Susan C. Ivy, William H. Kautz, Cynthia A. Kroll, Stephen Levy, Richard B. Mickley, Peter D. Miller, Charles T. Rainey, and Jack E. Van Zandt. 1977. *Earthquake prediction, uncertainty, and policies for the future—A technology assessment of earthquake prediction.* Menlo Park, CA: Stanford Research Institute, Center for Resource and Environmental Studies.

Whitlock, Craig, and Bob Williams. 1996. Damage may top $4 billion. *Raleigh News and Observer,* September 15, A1.

Wilma, David. 2001. Fat Tuesday violence in Pioneer Square kills one man on February 27, 2001. http://www.historylink.org/essays/output.cfm?file_id=3038 (accessed December 3, 2005).

Wilson, James Q. 1973. *Political organizations.* New York: Basic Books.

Woodlief, Wayne. 2001. Our brave new world requires change. *Boston Herald,* September 18, 39.

Work, Paul A., Jr., Spencer M. Rodgers, and Robert Osborne. 1999. Flood retrofit of coastal residential structures: Outer Banks, North Carolina. *Journal of Water Resources Planning and Management* 125 (2): 88–93.

index